Swimming Through You[r]

A unique programme of exercises to help [keep you healthy]
during pregnancy, to help prepare for labour and to get back in shape
after the birth.

(4) Lower Body Waterworks
- (i) Back Kicking & Relaxing
  - Flutter Kicks (easy + hard)
- (ii) Medley of Kicks
  - 10 Frog kicks
  - 10 Side Scissors kicks
  - 10 Frog kicks
  - 10 Side Scissors kicks
- (iii) Bicycle Pedal (on back)
- (iv) Leg Scissors (on back)
- (v) Leg & Inner Thigh Extension (side to wall)
- (vi) Calf & Ankle Stretches (tip toes)
- (vii) Wide Knee Bends
- (viii) Water Ballet Barre Exercises — leg lifts
   lower leg stretch
   leg swirl
- (ix) Wall Walk
- (x) Water Kegel
- (xi) Lamaze Tailor Sit

(5) Total Body Waterworks
- (i) Bobbing with Acqua Joggin
- (ii) Arm & Leg Stretch
- (iii) Leg Bend & Stretch (side to wall)
- (iv) Side Kick & Touch (side to wall)
- (v) Floating with Safe Recovery
- (vi) Pendulum body swing
- (vii) Treading
- (viii) Pike's Pull
- (ix) Posture check
- (x) Effleurage

Also by Jane Katz

SWIMMING FOR TOTAL FITNESS: A PROGRESSIVE AEROBIC PROGRAM
(with Nancy Bruning)

Swimming Through Your Pregnancy

The perfect exercise for pregnant women

Jane Katz Ed.D.

THORSONS PUBLISHERS LIMITED
Wellingborough, Northamptonshire

First published 1983 by Dolphin Books/Doubleday & Co. Inc.

First UK edition 1985

© JANE KATZ 1983

This book is sold subject to the condition that it shall not, by way of trade or otherwise, be lent, re-sold, hired out, or otherwise circulated without the publisher's prior consent in any form of binding or cover other than that in which it is published and without a similar condition including this condition being imposed on the subsequent purchaser.

British Library Cataloguing in Publication Data

Katz, Jane
 Swimming through your pregnancy.
 1. Swimming for women   2. Pregnancy
 I. Title
 613.7'1   RG558.7

ISBN 0-7225-0951-0

Printed and bound in Great Britain

To all parents, particularly mine, Dorothea and Leon, who introduced their children as well as thousands of people, both young and young at heart, to the wonderful world of water.

Foreword

Swimming is probably the best all-around exercise. It is especially well suited to the needs of the pregnant woman.

Pregnancy induces dramatic physical and mental changes in a woman. More and more, expectant mothers are responding to these changes with a desire to maintain fitness during pregnancy and to prepare themselves for labor and delivery. As a result, prepared childbirth programs have become popular; but although such programs help teach the expectant mother about her pregnancy and train her for labor, they are not sufficient. A pregnant woman will benefit from following an appropriate swimming program during the nine months prior to her delivery.

This important book sets forth the swimming program developed by Jane Katz, which is specifically designed to meet the needs of the pregnant woman during the course of her pregnancy. The techniques employed in the swimming program are safe and easy to learn, and they avoid overly strenuous or dangerous exercises. I recommend this book to all pregnant women. Only a very small minority of pregnant women will find themselves barred from Jane Katz's program for medical reasons.

Twenty years ago when I delivered my first baby, as was the practice, the young mother was unconscious—heavily sedated and then anesthetized. For some time after the birth both mother and newborn required careful supervision and some assistance with breathing.

Fortunately the practice has changed, as a result of medical advances and the increasing sophistication of women. Today many women minimize the use of anesthetics during labor and delivery, to help protect the health of their newborns and so that they can participate more actively in the birth process. Beneficial as this change is, it places increased demands on the mother. The swimming program set forth in this book can help to prepare the mother to meet those demands.

Jane Katz's lifelong interest and expertise in swimming becomes apparent when one reads this book. It is interesting and easy to follow. Her enthusiasm is obvious.

I congratulate the author on this book.

Desider J. Rothe, M.D.
Clinical Associate Professor
Obstetrics and Gynecology
New York Hospital
Cornell Medical Center

Acknowledgments

I was inspired to write this book by those wonderful women who swam and stayed fit during and after their pregnancies.

I'd like to give special thanks to:

My parents, Dorothea and Leon, who introduced me to the wonders of the water at an early age.

My sisters, Elaine Kuperberg and June Guzman, who swam through and after their pregnancies, and to their children, Stephen, Jason, and Justin.

My brother, Paul, for sharing his expertise in swimming.

Mark Rosenman for his continuous support, efforts, and expertise.

Desider J. Rothe, M.D., Clinical Associate Professor of Obstetrics and Gynecology, and Mona Shangold, M.D., Assistant Professor of Obstetrics and Gynecology, and Director, Sports Gynecology Center, both of the New York Hospital–Cornell Medical Center, for their professional guidance and contributions.

Elaine Hochuli, M.A., Recreation Specialist; Constance M. Gold, R.N., M.A., A.S.P.O. Lamaze Childbirth Specialist; Howard Chislett, Ed.D.; and Helen B. Pennoyer, M.S.W., A.S.P.O. Prepared Childbirth Instructor, for their valuable input and assistance.

Susan Schwartz, my editor, and Cathy Fowler, her assistant, for their enthusiasm, support, and encouragement.

Zvi Barak, Ph.D., Dan Drew, M.D., Herbert L. Erlanger, M.D., Farida Gadalla, M.D., Stephen B. Kurtin, M.D., Janet Mines, R.P.T., Willibald Nagler, M.D., and Thomas Verny, M.D., for their advice and comments.

Gerard Helferich, Lindy Hess, Mona Mark, illustrator, Alex Gotfryd, Doug Bergstreser, Sam Vaughan, and the entire staff of Doubleday & Company, for their efforts.

Pat Berlin, Angela Buchanan, Wendy Bogliogli, Jill Clayburgh, Joyce Bloom, Barbara Crossen, Joan Grossman, Cindy Kurtin, Linda Lebsack, Gaby Lehrer, Marcy Miller, Louise Neiman, Jan Stickley, Ruth Stern, Joy Taylor, Nancy Weiman, Rosemary Young, and my students at Bronx Community College, and many fitness and Masters swimmers, for sharing their swimming experiences during and after their pregnancies.

Carole Andrews, Susan Caton, Gregory Cilek, Cindy Clevenger, Don DeBolt, Pat Earle, Margaret Swan-Forbes, Mary Ann Jasien, the Princeton Y, Margaret Johnson, Anita Karabelas, Millie Leinweber, Manhattan Plaza, Paris and Waterside Health and Swim Clubs, Suzanne Michelle, Carol Miller, Jon S. Netts, the American National Red Cross, Marcellino Rodriguez, Michael Ross, Ph.D., Aerobics West, Susan Schaefer, Tony Staffieri, Nick Stringas, Holly Turner, and Sue Welch, for all their help.

And finally, to the many women and swim tots who inspired, swam, and worked with me. Many thanks to you all!

PUBLISHER'S AND AUTHOR'S COMMENT:

This swimming program is to be followed under
the supervision and guidance of your doctor
and it is not a substitute for consulting
your physician.

Contents

	FOREWORD	vii
	1 Introduction	1
I	STROKES	
	2 Introduction: Review of Your Swim Strokes in Relation to Your Pregnancy	13
	3 Reviewing Stroke Basics	15
	4 Crawl Stroke	16
	5 Breaststroke	23
	6 Backstroke	30
	7 Sidestroke	39
	8 Stroke Cues Chart	46
	9 Push-offs and Turns	47
II	WATERWORKS EXERCISES	
	10 Introduction to Waterworks	55
	11 Breathing Waterworks	58
	12 Upper Body Waterworks	63
	13 Middle Body Waterworks	68
	14 Lower Body Waterworks	73
	15 Total Body Waterworks	80
	16 At-Home Waterworks	86
III	PREGNANCY SWIM PROGRAM	
	17 Introduction	93
	18 Trimester 1	100
	19 Trimester 2	116
	20 Trimester 3	141

IV	POSTPARTUM PROGRAM		
	21	Introduction	163
	22	Twelve-Week Progressive Swim Program	166
	23	Introduction to Synchronized Swimming (Water Ballet)	189
	24	Introductory Diving Progression	202
	25	Introductory Butterfly Skills	204
V	FAMILY SWIM TIPS		
	26	Introduction	209
	27	Water Play with Your Newborn – Do Go Near the Water!	211
	28	Infants	213
	29	Toddler Stage – The Terrible Two's	217
	30	Preschoolers	220
	31	Youngsters – Age Six to Teens	222
VI	COMMON Q's AND UNCOMMON A's		
	32	Swimming During Your Pregnancy	225
	33	About Health, Beauty, and Safety Q's	228
	34	Postpartum Period	231
	35	Family and Baby Swim Q's	234
	INDEX		241

Swimming Through Your Pregnancy

1

Introduction

Personal Comments

"I felt terrific after swimming."

"I felt a sense of accomplishment and mental satisfaction that I could continue swimming during my pregnancy. It was so pleasurable, and beneficial as well."

"Swimming helped ease my fatigue and relax me, and the buoyancy of the water gave my body a rest."

"I felt swimming benefited both baby and me."

"I'm certain that swimming during my first pregnancy with the twins had much to do with the ease and speed of delivery."

"Labor, after all, is in many ways really an 'athletic event,' and swimming helps to keep you in shape for 'the event.'"

The women who made these statements all have something in common: they benefited from swimming through their pregnancies.

You can join the growing number of women who prepare for childbirth by keeping themselves fit and healthy, without stress or strain. This book tells all you need to know about how, when, and where you can *swim through your pregnancy*.

Introduction: Before You Take the Plunge

Congratulations! In a few months' time you will become a new mother. Obviously you're curious about this book, *Swimming Through*

Your Pregnancy, which tells you how to swim through your pregnancy. The suggestion that you swim through your pregnancy may strike you as a bit unusual, as well as daring, but think about it for a moment. Pregnancy, as we now know, is not a debilitating condition. Many women continue their daily activities while pregnant. Although our Victorian past had disposed us to believe that pregnant women should lessen their activities during the nine months of pregnancy, medical science advises today's pregnant women to continue their normal routines. In fact, many obstetricians now encourage their patients to engage in some form of physical conditioning, believing that a woman whose body is in good physical condition will be less likely to have difficulty during labor and childbirth. Women who have not been physically active prior to pregnancy now are being encouraged to begin programs of physical conditioning as soon as possible.

This book will help you enjoy your pregnancy and prepare for labor and delivery by teaching you how to tone and strengthen your body—gently—through swimming and other water exercises. Not only will your labor and delivery be easier, and your pregnancy more enjoyable, but after you give birth, your recovery and return to fitness and figure will be quicker!

If you were an active person prior to your pregnancy, you already know about the benefits of exercise—vitality, strength, flexibility, weight control, and relaxation. What you probably don't know is that by following this swimming program during your pregnancy, you can continue to enjoy all of these benefits safely as you prepare for childbirth.

Of course, you should not begin this program without the approval of your doctor, and your doctor should be kept advised of your activity throughout your pregnancy.

If you think your doctor will object to your swimming during your pregnancy, you're in for a pleasant surprise! Why? Because more and more obstetricians are encouraging mothers-to-be to engage in fitness programs both for the mother's sake and for the sake of the unborn child. These doctors know that the right kind of exercise will strengthen the muscles you will use during the birth process and will improve your cardio-aerobic fitness, facilitating your breathing during labor and delivery. (Cardio-aerobic fitness results from a strong heart and lungs, efficient circulation, and efficient oxygen utilization.) They know that improving your ability to utilize oxygen during your pregnancy may directly benefit your unborn child by providing more oxygen for prenatal development. And swimming is the best fitness activity you can find! Swimming is a unique exercise because it simultaneously improves your cardio-aerobic fitness, strength, and flexibility, while avoiding stress and strain. In addition, the

INTRODUCTION 3

buoyancy of the water gives you support and reduces the energy expenditure necessary for a given exercise activity, so that you can exercise with more ease. The result is the maintenance of optimal fitness with less fatigue and exhaustion.

You'll discover that swimming is a perfect exercise for you during and after your pregnancy. It involves a minimum of stress and no pounding or straining at all. Plus, the medium itself—water—is absolutely delightful! Its buoyancy will help support you and its soothing properties will relax you. Just think, you'll have that weightless feeling, which you will welcome as your body begins to expand.

An additional note about weight control: a mother-to-be can expect to gain from 20 to 30 pounds during a normal pregnancy.° Most of this weight usually is gained during the second and third trimesters of pregnancy, although a weight gain may begin immediately. Approximately 16 of these pounds can be attributed to the weight of the baby, the amniotic sac and fluid, the expanded uterus, the placenta, and the increase in the mother's blood supply. The balance of weight is due to the normal accumulation of fat and body fluids. This weight, in most cases, is shed with little or no difficulty shortly after delivery. However, any weight gain over 30 pounds is usually excess fat, which the mother will retain after birth. For most women, this excess weight can only be lost through great determination and effort.

Doctors and nutritionists stress that a proper diet during your pregnancy is very important, both to protect your health and to assure proper prenatal development of the baby. Eating less to lose weight is generally not recommended for pregnant women. A proper swimming program will help keep off excess pounds during your pregnancy without ill-advised dieting. Your pregnancy will be easier (not to mention safer) if you don't have to lug around excess fat or feel that you have to deprive yourself every time you sit down to eat. You can find some general suggestions concerning nutrition in chapter 35 of this book.

What Happens During Pregnancy: Bodily Changes

Before proceeding to the program itself, let's take a brief look at pregnancy and perhaps dispel some of the myths and fallacies that surround it.

° It is important to note here that patients who have been told that their pregnancy is threatened or is at risk *should not start any exercise program.* Although the number of women who fall into this category is small, it is imperative that you check with your doctor before beginning this or any other exercise program.

Pregnancy involves changes in every part of your body. The most obvious, of course, is the increase in the size of your uterus.

Your uterus is a muscle (and what a muscle!) that increases in strength and thickness as pregnancy progresses. Your uterus is comprised of three distinct layers of muscle, each of which plays a specific role in labor and in delivery. During pregnancy, your uterus changes dramatically in both size and shape, requiring other muscles to maintain it in proper position. For example, ligaments known as the broad ligaments act like giant elastic bands to keep your uterus safely suspended in the middle of your pelvis. Surrounding your uterus are abdominal and pelvic floor muscles, which will assist during labor and delivery. If your abdominal muscles are too weak to support the changes in your body's center of gravity as your unborn child develops, you may find yourself changing your posture to compensate for this weakness. The end result will be lower back pains and general discomfort. Good abdominal muscle tone will provide the needed support and will also help maintain the integrity and function of your intestines and other organs as they are displaced by your growing uterus.

As your pregnancy progresses, your weight increases, and your center of gravity changes, additional strains will be placed on your back, hips, and legs. This can result in some discomfort. Swimming can help to strengthen muscles in these areas, easing the problem.

Surrounding your uterus is a bone structure known as the pelvic girdle, which helps direct your uterus and acts as the "funnel" through which your baby must travel during birth. Improved muscle tone of your back, hips, legs, and ligaments will help maintain the attitude of your pelvic girdle in relation to the rest of your body and promote joint flexibility necessary to accommodate your swelling uterus.

During your pregnancy, your breasts become larger and heavier in preparation for breast-feeding. Proper exercise, especially swimming, will strengthen the chest muscles that help support your breasts.

During labor and delivery, you will have to relax your pelvic muscles to enable your baby to pass through the birth canal. This swimming program will help you gain more control over these muscles so that you can relax them when necessary. It will also give you more strength and control of your abdominal and pelvic floor muscles, which can be of vital assistance when you are required to push.

Your blood supply will increase from 25 to 50 percent during your pregnancy. Your heart may even beat a little faster than it did before pregnancy. Obviously, this will impose additional demands on your heart. Your heart will be able to handle these demands with greater ease if it is strengthened through a sensible swimming program. In addition, your improved cardiac efficiency may help to minimize swelling in your lower extremities, varicose veins, and hemorrhoids, which commonly attend pregnancy.

Myths: What Great-grandmother Thought

Now let's look at a few myths concerning pregnancy and pursuing a physical fitness program:

MYTH: Exercise can harm a woman's reproductive organs.
FACT: A proper exercise program has no adverse effects on a woman's reproductive organs. A woman's uterus is a very well protected organ, guarded by strong ligaments and surrounded by the pelvic bone.

MYTH: Exercise during pregnancy is dangerous to the unborn child.
FACT: This myth is based on the misconception that moderate movement or bending during a normal pregnancy will in some way harm the unborn child. This is completely inaccurate. The unborn child is well protected from injury by the abdominal wall and the strong uterine muscle (both of which will be strengthened by using this swimming program), as well as by the amniotic fluid and sac.

The Wonderful Water: Why Swim During Your Pregnancy?

Many of us are familiar with the following line from *The Ancient Mariner:* "Water, water everywhere. . . ." Indeed, water is all around us—70 percent of the earth's surface is covered with it, and most of the world's population is clustered in coastal areas. Life, it is said, began in the water, and life would cease without water. Man is inherently drawn to water. If you don't believe me, just check out any beach near any city on a hot summer day! Man is not alone in his need for water—animals and plants need it to survive. Without water, all life would cease to exist. Man and other animals can survive for long periods of time without eating solid food, but deprive them of water and they perish in a very short time. Man and other animals are naturally drawn to water for their survival, their cures, and their play.

Historically, water has been used by many peoples as a curative and in the practice of their religions. Ritualistic bathing probably predates ancient Egypt. The ancient Greeks developed the communal bath and, of course, the Romans borrowed and elaborated on the idea. The Romans enjoyed their baths and wherever the Romans went in the ancient world, a bath was soon to follow. When the Romans invaded Britain, they made good use of the hot springs at Bath, which they named *Aquae Sulis*. Europe is the site of many natural hot springs, the most famous being the mineral springs at Spa in Belgium. These springs are so famous that the word spa is now a part of many languages. In America, Warm Springs in Georgia became a famous site for treating victims of polio in the 1930s and 1940s, for it was here that President Franklin D. Roosevelt had gone for treatment after he contracted the disease.

During the eighteenth and nineteenth centuries, there developed in Europe and in America a health movement that used water in the treatment of illness and injury. Hydrotherapy, as it was called, was based on the belief that water could help rid the body of the heat of fevers and could cure certain ailments by conducting heat to the body. Hydrotherapists claimed that water could be used to cure almost every ill, from allergies to typhoid fever. Today some of hydrotherapy's concepts and methods are still in use; for example, severely burned people may be treated with warm water to help the body to retain heat. Whirlpool baths are often used in the treatment of sports-related injuries.

Swimming is one of the oldest forms of physical activity. Throughout history and legend there have been heroic feats associated with swimming, such as Leander's nightly swim across the Hellespont to visit his beloved Hero. The English poet Lord Byron was so enthralled with this legend that he too swam across the Hellespont. John F. Kennedy became a hero by saving some of his wounded crew from drowning when their PT boat was torpedoed during World War II.

Swimming, along with other water exercises, is *the best* exercise for almost everybody, but especially for *you* during your pregnancy. More important, it is a gentle and progressive exercise that does not subject your body to pounding, twisting, or straining.

Swimming strengthens your cardiovascular and skeletal muscle systems, it helps control your weight, and it makes you feel good. Your cardiovascular system carries blood to and from all parts of your body via the heart, arteries, and veins. Exercise actually strengthens the arteries, especially the coronary artery; it can lower the level of fat in your blood; and it often lowers blood pressure. A healthy cardiovascular system is vitally important to you, the mother-to-be, because blood, rich in oxygen, must be efficiently transported throughout your body to the placenta, which provides your baby with oxygen and nourishment.

Swimming is unparalleled in helping you achieve overall fitness and relaxation. Swimming tones and strengthens your arms, shoulders, abdomen, back, hips, and legs, and it does these things all at once. Swimming promotes flexibility, especially in the pelvic area. It is a wonderful way to burn up extra calories and it helps you to avoid any excess weight gain. For example, if you swim a quarter to a half a mile in twenty minutes, you will use up 300 or more calories.

Swimming has several other advantages over other forms of exercise. There is minimal chance of overheating while swimming because of the cooling properties of the water. Swimming is done in a horizontal position, which can aid respiration by removing the weight of the womb from your diaphragm. The support provided by water facilitates blood flow, and it helps to relieve pressure exerted on the bladder and pelvic organs by the womb.

Naturally, your swimming program should be tempered to fit the stage of your pregnancy. This book, together with your doctor's guidance, will show you how to adjust your swimming program to your pregnancy as it progresses from trimester to trimester.

You should always follow your doctor's advice, and you should always *listen to your body!* If you experience any muscular discomfort while exercising, taper off. If you experience any pain, or if muscular discomfort persists, see your doctor. The idea is to make your swimming program fit *your* needs.

You'll find that swimming is good for your mind as well as for your body. Water is, of itself, a very sensuous medium. While immersed in it, you seemingly defy gravity—you're suspended. Your spirits are lifted as much as your body. Water eases tension and pleases your soul.

How Much Should You Swim?

How much you should swim during your pregnancy depends on several factors, including your general physical condition, the stage of your pregnancy, your doctor's advice, and your body's signals.

As a general rule, it is best to swim approximately three times per week for twenty to thirty minutes per session. Space your swims evenly throughout the week. Start off slowly. First time exercisers have a tendency to overdo it when they begin a program—don't strain. If swimming three times per week seems like too much, try swimming two times per week—even once a week is fine if that is what is comfortable for you. Your motto should be, *Moderation.*

Try to swim at a regular time—in the morning if you're an early bird, in the evening if you're a night owl. If you are working and there are facilities close by, a swim at lunchtime is a perfect "pick-me-up"!

During the early stages of pregnancy, and depending on how you feel, you should be able to swim fairly energetically with no discomfort. As your pregnancy progresses into its later stages, your swimming should become less demanding. Even during the later stages of your pregnancy, you will find that the exercises in this book are most beneficial and enjoyable. You'll be strengthening your body—not straining it! As you approach term, simply sitting or floating in the water will do wonders for your comfort and your state of mind.

Swimming and Childbirth

Water, as I've pointed out, has long been used to promote well-being in the body. Did you know that it is used as a medium to make the birth process less traumatic? The Russians, for example, have successfully experimented with delivering babies in water, and perhaps this technique will find wider applicability in the near future. Leboyer, the French obstetrician, developed the celebrated childbirth technique of "birth without violence," which eases the transition of the newborn from womb to world by massaging the newborn in lukewarm water immediately following delivery.

If you are planning to practice prepared childbirth, such as the Lamaze technique, you'll find that this swimming program will complement your childbirth program. Many prepared childbirth methods train the mother-to-be in how to use her abdominal, pelvic, and uterine muscles in delivery. If these muscles have been strengthened by practicing this program, the usefulness of the childbirth training will be enhanced. In addition, prepared childbirth methods emphasize rhythmic breathing techniques. These breath techniques will be enhanced by this swimming program, since the fundamental skill of swimming is rhythmic breathing. Proper breathing technique also increases your aerobic capacity. This swimming program has adapted some prepared childbirth exercises into your swimming-through-pregnancy program. Even if you deliver your baby by Cesarean section, your childbirth will be easier for you if you're in good physical condition. If you prepare yourself by swimming, you will be stronger during your labor and delivery and you'll be more comfortable and more relaxed.

At this point I would like to elaborate a little more on prepared childbirth, specifically the Lamaze Method. The Lamaze Method is an adaptation of two schools of thought. The first is based on the Pavlovian theory of the conditioned response, that is, when a mother is in labor, she will be able to exercise control over her body during a contraction. The second school of thought is the "fear-tension-pain" theory suggested by the English doctor Grantly Dick-Read. Dick-Read maintained that the more one is educated and informed, the less one will fear the unknown of impending labor and delivery. With lessened fear, there will be lessened tension, and with lessened tension there will be less pain. The Lamaze Method simply adopted these theories and added some sound physiological principles that combine to make a childbirth technique for the various stages of labor. As this swimming program unfolds, you will see how the Lamaze Method relates quite well to the benefits of swimming and the water.

General Swimming Safety Tips

Swim only with your doctor's approval.
Listen to your body.
Never swim alone.
Swim in water that is warm (about 80° F). The air temperature should be within 5° F of the water's temperature.
Swim when the facility is not too crowded; swimming should not be a contact sport!
Use moderation in your swimming program.

How to Use This Book

This book details a unique swimming program to be used during your pregnancy, postpartum, and with your new baby.

Part I of this book begins with a swim, stroke, and tips review. It describes how you will adjust your swimming skills as your needs change from trimester to trimester.

Part II describes Waterworks exercises for total body fitness along with at-home water exercises.

Part III provides a swimming program for each trimester of your pregnancy. Within each swim session, there are three levels, geared to your specific needs and swimming ability.

Part IV of this book will give you a postpartum swimming program to hasten your recovery and to help you regain your fitness. It includes synchronized swimming and other aquatic skills.

Part V includes guidelines for family swimming, plus introducing your newborn to the wonders of the water.

The final part of this book contains answers to commonly asked questions, including some about health, safety, cosmetic care, nutrition, and where to find appropriate swim equipment.

Now, turn the page, suit up, and take the plunge into your personal pregnancy swimming program.

Welcome to the wonderful world of the water!

I

Strokes

2

Introduction: Review of Your Swim Strokes in Relation to Your Pregnancy

Although you may not be vying for an Olympic medal, you can always add to your present knowledge and level of skill. Whether you're a recreational swimmer or an avid fitness swimmer, the following swim tips and exercises are designed to help you to enjoy your swimming throughout your pregnancy; they also provide a wide variety of strokes, which you will find useful both during and after your pregnancy.

Swimming is a science and it is also an art. When you swim, you not only exercise your body; you also exercise your mind and your soul.

Depending on your skill level, you may wish to relearn, review, refine, or actually learn for the first time all of your swim skills. If you are a novice swimmer, you can use the "Waterworks" exercises as part of your main swim session.

Principles of Movement in the Water

Buoyancy: The specific gravity of water is 1.0. Your specific gravity is less, meaning you will float. As your pregnancy advances, your specific gravity will change and you'll become more buoyant.

Body Position: Good body mechanics are essential for everyday life. They are particularly important during your pregnancy because it is at this time that there is a shift in your center of gravity; this puts added pressure on areas of your body that may not be subject to excessive strain under normal circumstances. Because of this change, you may have a tendency to be off balance. So take it easy.

Newton's Third Law of Motion: In short, for every action, there is an equal and opposite reaction; e.g., when you push against the water, you propel yourself forward.

3

Reviewing Stroke Basics

Each stroke will consist of the following parts:

Body Position: All strokes begin and are maintained in a specific body position. This is important for your comfort and relaxation.

Breathing: Good breathing skills will help you maintain a good aerobic fitness level during your pregnancy.

Arm Motion: No matter how different they may seem, all of the arm strokes in this section share the following elements:

> THE CATCH: This is the starting point of your arm in the water.
>
> THE PULL: This is the propulsion stage where you push water backward in order to go forward.
>
> THE RECOVERY: This is where you rest and return your arm to the catch position.

Leg Motion: The use of your hip and thigh muscles during the kick will develop power for labor and delivery.

Coordination: You will coordinate all of the above in each stroke for smooth, fluid movement.

4

Crawl Stroke

The crawl stroke is recommended throughout your pregnancy. The crawl is the fastest and most efficient stroke because of the angle of the arm. It is also the easiest to learn because the opposing leg and arm motions are similar to walking. The crawl is probably the first stroke you learned, but there is more to it than meets the eye, for example, the new S-shaped arm motion.

To refine your stroke technique, try this S-shaped pull, as well as other variations discussed in this book.

Body Position

Your body is prone (face down) in the water. Your body should have a long, relaxed feeling. It should be streamlined along its central axis (your spine), and the water level should come between your eyebrows and your hairline.

Arm Motion

The arm motion consists of three parts: the *catch*, the *pull*, and the *recovery*. The catch and the pull make up the *stroke*. The catch begins each stroke with the hand extended under the water's surface. The

CRAWL STROKE 17

stroke begins with the catch and continues into the pull. Your hand enters the water at a 30° to 40° angle. Your arm then is extended fully into the water, at which point the pull begins. The pull is done by pressing the water downward and backward, toward your thighs, keeping your hand close to your thigh at the finish of the press. The pull is what propels you through the water. The recovery follows the pull when your arm lifts out of the water and returns to the starting catch position. Keep your elbow higher than your hand during the recovery.

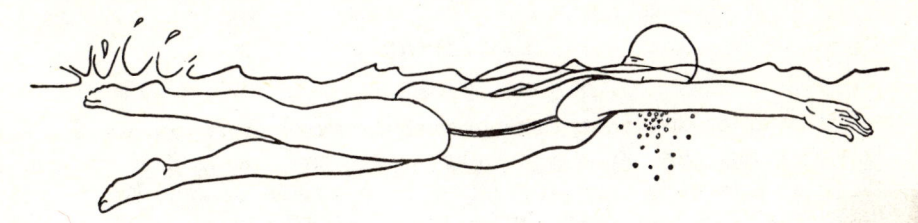

The crawl stroke. The catch: Extend one arm above head.

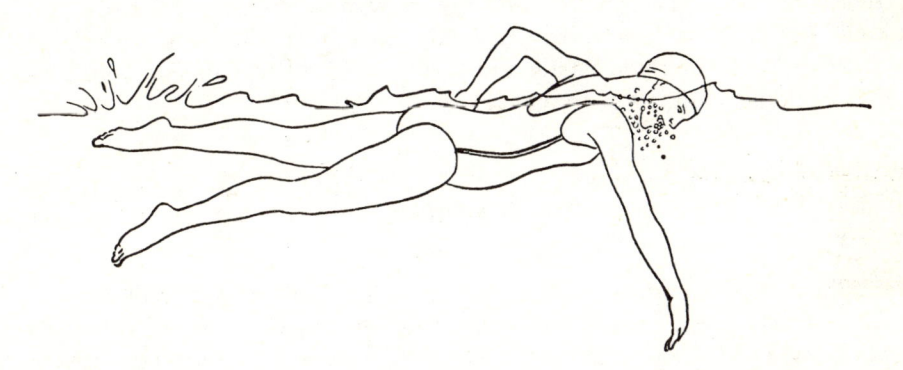

The pull: Pull arm downward and backward through water until hand is close to thigh.

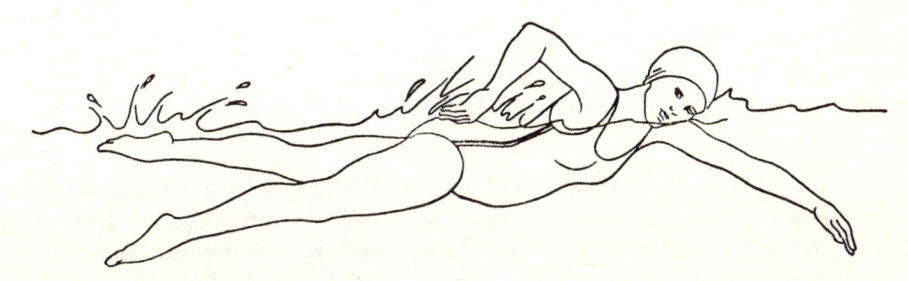

The recovery: Lift arm out of water and return to overhead catch position.

Body Roll

As one arm recovers, there is a natural tendency for the body to roll almost 45° toward the arm that is pulling. This is a natural and advantageous action and it should not be resisted.

Leg Motion

The flutter kick is the leg motion for the crawl stroke. For the flutter kick, your legs move up and down as if you were walking. The action of the kick comes from your hips and thighs. Your knees should be slightly flexed, but your ankles should be loose and relaxed for comfort and efficiency. Rather than overkicking and splashing, you should just make the water "boil." The kick is used primarily to stabilize your stroke and body position. As your pregnancy advances, you will find your body changing so that as you inhale and turn your head to one side your legs may be doing a scissors or trudgen kick.

Breathing

Rhythmic breathing, which is the easiest and only correct way to continuously get air while doing the crawl, is done by turning your face to one side of the water to inhale, then returning it back into the water to exhale. Use both your nose and mouth for inhalation and exhalation. If you don't breathe properly, you will tire easily, because you'll run out of breath.

Coordinating Rhythmic Breathing and Arm Motion

To breathe rhythmically and to coordinate the arm motion of the crawl stroke, follow the "law of opposites." As you turn your head to one side to inhale, you extend your arm forward on the opposite side, and your hand enters the water. The arm on your breathing side is back and ready to recover.

Special Crawl Stroke Arm Exercises for Use During and After Your Pregnancy

The following exercises are designed to give you upper arm strength, which will help you during pushing; they will introduce timing, which is important if you are into natural childbirth, where timing is an essential part of the birth process.

CATCH-UP CRAWL ARM STROKE: As you do the crawl stroke, touch the thumb of one hand to the thumb on the other hand as your arms are extended in front of you, before starting your next arm motion.

• First practice on land, then in shallow water, and then walking in chest-deep water. Touching your thumbs together slows your stroke so that you can concentrate on each arm motion.

The S-pull for the crawl stroke.

- Swim half a lap of catch-up stroke, then finish the lap with regular crawl stroke.
- Swim an entire lap of catch-up.
- Alternate laps of catch-up with the crawl stroke.

STROKE COUNT: Count the number of arm strokes you use to complete one lap while pulling. Then try to decrease this number on consecutive laps.

TRY YOUR S-SHAPED PULL: This will help to strengthen your upper body as well as increase the efficiency of your swimming. To practice, first stand in chest-deep water and extend both arms in front of you below the surface. Then trace a question mark with your right hand by pulling first outward, then inward toward your hip, and then pressing backward. To recover, bend your elbow and point it to the sky, lift your arm out of the water, and touch your thumbs together in front of you. Repeat the process with your left hand (tracing a reverse question mark). Use the S-shaped pull while swimming, remembering to alternate arms (as one pulls, the other recovers). This exercise is a good way to develop the muscles of your arms.

Special Crawl Stroke Leg Exercises for Use During and After Your Pregnancy

These exercises may be done with or without fins or a kickboard. They will help tone your legs and buttocks as well as strengthen your abdominal area. These exercises are great for overall body tone, and they will also stretch your muscles.

SIT AND KICK: Sit comfortably on the edge of the pool, with your weight shifted slightly backward, while dangling your feet in the water. Practice the flutter kick, keeping your ankles loose. Use your hip and thigh muscles.

PRONE WALL KICK: Standing in the water, face the pool wall, grasp the edge of the pool, with one hand and pull. Simultaneously place your other hand beneath the surface of the water, and push against the wall so that your body floats prone or face down. This is the "bracket" position. Flutter kick, just hard enough to make the water "boil." Your hips provide the power for the kick.

KICKBOARD KICK: Grasp the board with both hands, keeping your arms straight. The board will give you support while you practice your flutter

CRAWL STROKE

kick. This helps to strengthen your leg muscles, and you can do it with your head either in or out of the water.

BREATHE AND KICK: If you're having trouble with the flutter kick, try this. Hold a kickboard as you float face forward in the water. Practice your rhythmic breathing, and as you turn your head in the water to exhale, do a few flutter kicks. When you turn your head to the side to inhale, relax your legs.

In general, these exercises will help you to strengthen your legs and lower body muscles—this is especially helpful because these are some of the muscles you will be using during labor.

Special Crawl Stroke Breathing Exercises for Use During and After Your Pregnancy

These exercises will aid in developing your aerobic capacity.

THE WALKING CRAWL STROKE WITH RHYTHMIC BREATHING: Practice combining the crawl stroke arm motion and rhythmic breathing while walking in chest-deep water. (Remember the law of opposites.)

WALL KICK AND RHYTHMIC BREATHING: Hold on to the wall in the bracket position, and practice rhythmic breathing by inhaling on the side of your underwater arm. You may want to try adding your scissors kick or trudgen kick. You'll feel an extra stretch on the wall.

Crawl Stroke Tips and Special Benefits for Use During and After Your Pregnancy

Once you've mastered the crawl stroke, keep these pointers in mind to help you swim more easily:

1. Keep your body position stretched out and streamlined.

2. To get the most from each arm motion, stretch your arm out on the catch and complete the pull to your hip.

3. If you feel out of breath, stop and rest. Review rhythmic breathing to be sure that your air exchange is complete. You should avoid hyperventilation, that is, taking in too much oxygen and not exhaling enough oxygen.

4. When inhaling, rotate your head so that your nose and mouth just clear the water.

5. Use the S-shaped arm pull for the crawl stroke.

6. Don't overkick; this will tire you out, and it will also be uncomfortable. Adjust your kick accordingly.

7. Keep your elbows higher than your hands during the recovery.

8. Remember: Use your nose and mouth to inhale and use your nose and mouth to exhale, and breathe continuously. This technique is a good pattern to learn—it is similar to the breathing methods you'll learn if you attend a prepared childbirth course.

5

Breaststroke

This is an easy and relaxing stroke when swum slowly. It is a very popular stroke because of its relatively long and restful glide. In the breaststroke, the heart-shaped circular arm motion and the modified frog kick provide you with equal propulsion. This stroke is recommended throughout your pregnancy, particularly in your third trimester.

Body Position

Your body is extended in the prone (face down) position. At the beginning of your stroke (glide position), your arms are extended straight out in front of you. Your legs are extended straight out behind you, with your feet just below the surface. Always look in the direction you are swimming.

Arm Motion

In the breaststroke, your arms move simultaneously and symmetrically under the water during the entire stroke. As your arms move together they trace the outline of a heart during the pull phase of the arm motion. On the recovery, both arms are extended straight ahead under the water.

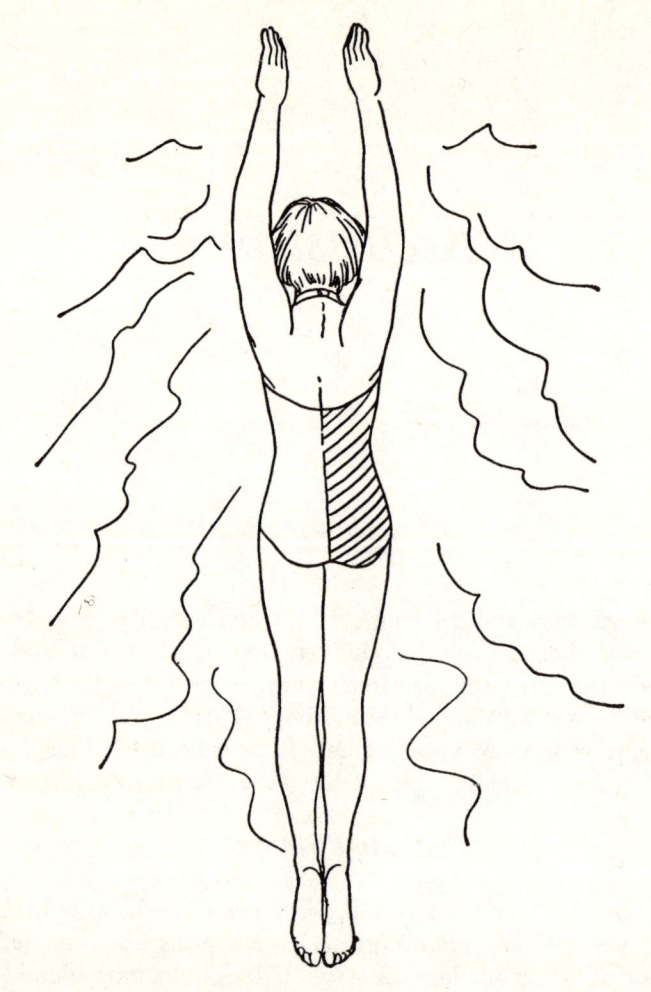

The breaststroke: Starting (catch) position.

The catch begins with your hands about as far apart as your shoulders. Rotate your wrists so that your palms face outward with your thumbs pointing downward so your hands can get a hold on the water.

During the pull keep your elbows higher than your hands. The most efficient pull ends approximately at your shoulders.

The recovery should be a smooth, natural motion. It continues at the end of the pull. Recover your hands with palms close together in a prayer position. Glide with your arms extended before the next stroke.

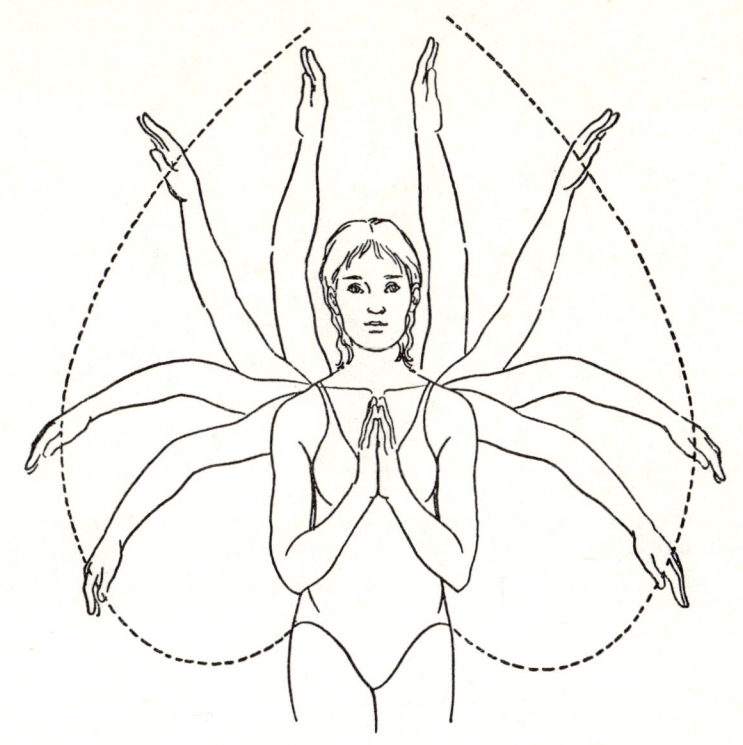

The pull: Pull arms simultaneously and symmetrically in heart-shaped movement under water.

Leg Motion

The frog kick is the most commonly used leg motion in the breaststroke. The frog kick, also known as the breaststroke kick, involves the following movements, performed while you are prone in the water. Spread your knees wider than your hips, and drop them slightly as you bring your heels together. Then extend your legs by straightening them at the knees while flexing your feet so that your legs form a wide V. Bring your legs (which should be straight at this point) together, while pointing your toes to complete the kick.

The recovery: Extend arms as you begin frog kick by spreading knees wider than hips and bending them slightly.

Breathing

Inhale when your head and shoulders rise as your arm pull widens; exhale as your face submerges and your arms recover to the glide position.

BREASTSTROKE 27

The glide: Extend legs, then push them together, keeping toes pointed and arms extended.

Coordinating Arm Motion, Leg Motion, and Breathing

The basic stroke sequence is: pull (inhale), kick, and glide (exhale). To initiate coordination of the breaststroke, begin the pull first and follow with the kick. Bend your knees to begin the kick, then continue both arm and leg motions simultaneously to finish the stroke, with your body fully extended and streamlined for the glide.

Special Breaststroke Arm Exercises
for Use During and After Your Pregnancy

These help you to strengthen your pectoral (chest) muscles.

WALKING BREASTSTROKE: Walk in chest-deep water practicing the heart-shaped arm motion—this exercise helps to develop and to expand your chest cavity.

STROKE COUNT: Count the number of arm strokes you do to complete a lap. On succeeding laps, try to decrease this number.

Special Breaststroke Leg Exercises
for Use During and After Your Pregnancy

During pregnancy, leg bulges may become more pronounced because of muscle atrophy and weight gain. The following leg exercises help to condition and tone your muscles. This conditioning and toning is also useful during the postpartum period. The muscles used in the frog kick are for the most part the same as those used in the leg-raising and tailor-sitting exercises done in prepared childbirth classes.

SIT AND KICK: Practice the frog kick while sitting on the pool deck with your legs lowered in the water.

KICKBOARD KICK: Extend your arms straight in front of you and grasp a kickboard. Either keep your head above water and breathe normally or coordinate inhalation and exhalation with the kick.

WALL KICK: Assume the bracket position (one hand at water line, one hand below surface against wall) and practice your kick.

VERTICAL KICK: While sculling (see p. 31) in the water, practice the frog kick while in a vertical position.

Special Breaststroke Breathing Exercises
for Use During Your Pregnancy

Lamaze breathing techniques, which you'll be learning at about the seventh month in preparation for labor and delivery, may be employed while swimming the breaststroke. You'll be doing more of these in your childbirth classes:

THE CLEANSING BREATH: This can be done before and after every lap or set of laps. Inhale through your nose and exhale through your mouth.

FIRST STAGE OF EARLY LABOR BREATHING TECHNIQUE: You will be breathing six to nine times per minute.

Breaststroke Tips and Special Benefits for Use During and After Your Pregnancy

1. You have greater visibility with this stroke (since you are always looking forward). You can feel more relaxed and confident because you know where you are in relation to the other swimmers.
2. The ideal pull is at shoulder width in a diagonally downward position.
3. Inhale when your head and shoulders rise naturally above the water as a result of your pull.
4. Be as streamlined and relaxed as possible during the glide.
5. To stretch and tone your upper body, emphasize your heart-shaped arm motion.
6. The frog kick is similar to the Lamaze tailor-sitting position, which helps strengthen and tone inner thigh muscles.
7. As your pregnancy progresses and you become more buoyant, your feet may break the surface more often in the frog kick. If they do, try dropping your knees farther down before extending them into the V position.
8. As your abdomen increases in size, it is nice to have a floating sensation for a while.

6

Backstroke

There are many backstroke variations, for example, alternating arm pulls and the S-pull pattern. Breathing during this stroke is relatively easy since you're swimming on your back and therefore your nose and mouth are out of the water. There is one caveat about the backstroke to keep in mind—you can't see where you're going, so be careful.

The backstroke skills are presented according to arm motions from smaller to larger, with increasing difficulty. They include: sculling, elementary backstroke, inverted breaststroke, and the windmill backstroke. The flutter kick or breaststroke kick (frog kick) is used with sculling and the elementary backstroke; for the windmill, use the flutter kick; for the inverted breaststroke, use the modified kick.

Body Position

Your body is floating face up (supine) with your legs extended. Your chin should be tipped slightly forward, and your eyes should be looking diagonally toward your feet. Your general body position will vary according to your stroke and the stage of your pregnancy.

Breathing

Even though your face is out of the water, your breathing should be rhythmic. You should continuously inhale and exhale while on your back, especially when practicing specific childbirth breathing techniques you will be using later on.

Sculling

ARMS: Sculling uses arm movements similar to the ones used in treading water. To practice, place your arms in front of you at waist level, parallel to the pool's bottom, with your thumbs up and your palms facing each other. Now make a figure eight motion (like an infinity sign) with each hand. Holding your hands at about waist level, turn your thumbs down and press your arms out away from each other until they're about shoulder width apart; then turn your thumbs up again and press your arms toward each other until the palms touch. Now, transfer this movement to hip level, moving inward and outward. Remember to point your fingers upward by flexing your wrist, which will help in propulsion.

LEGS: Use either an easy flutter kick or breaststroke kick while sculling.

COORDINATION: Your arms and legs should move continuously.

The Elementary Backstroke

ARMS: To begin, your arms should be straight and at your sides. This is the *resting* or *glide* position. Now slide your fingertips along your sides up to your underarms for the recovery. Exend your arms outward from the shoulders, beneath the surface of the water, with your palms facing downward in a T position for the catch. Pause for a moment before pressing your arms straight downward to your outer thighs for the pull (the power part of the stroke). Hold your arms in this glide position momentarily before you begin the cycle again.

Elementary backstroke: Starting and glide position.

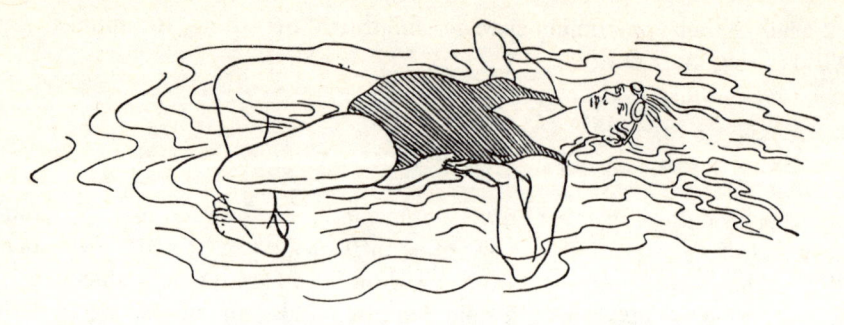

The recovery: Slide hands up to arm pits and begin frog kick.

The catch and pull: Extend arms outward and pull down to sides while completing frog kick.

LEGS: Use either the breaststroke kick or the flutter kick, on your back—whatever you're comfortable using.

COORDINATION: Coordinate the arm and leg motions in the following manner: Up on the recovery, out on the catch, together on the pull, and then glide.

The Inverted Breaststroke

The inverted breaststroke is a combination of the breaststroke and the elementary backstroke.

BACKSTROKE

ARMS: All arm movements are underwater. The arm stroke begins with your arms extended overhead in a glide position. The catch begins with your arms forming a V upward from the shoulders. From the catch position, the arms press outward and downward all the way until your hands touch your outer thighs. Your arms may be slightly bent or straight during the press. At the end of the press, you recover your hands by sliding them up the sides of your body, as in the elementary backstroke. Your hands then complete the overhead extension to begin the glide.

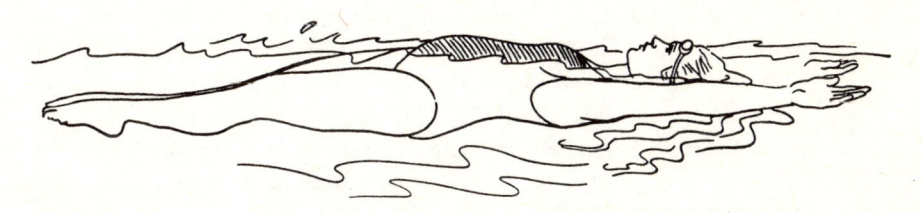

Inverted breaststroke. The catch: Extend arms overhead.

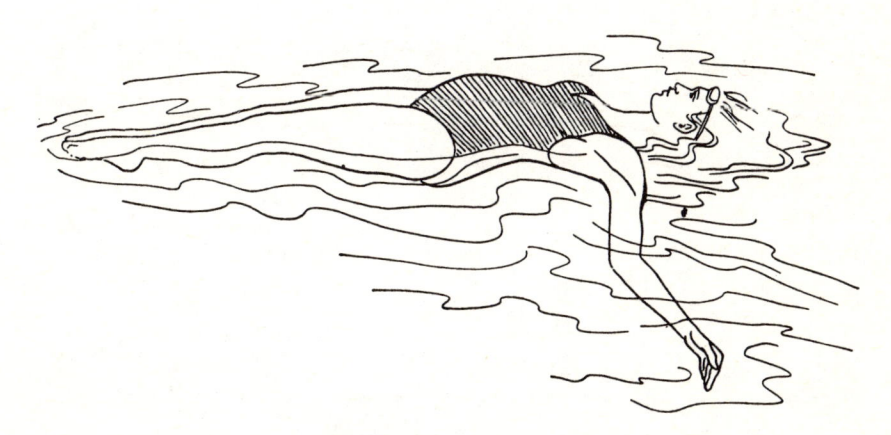

The pull: Press arms outward and downward toward thighs.

LEGS: Use the frog kick with any modification that is comfortable for you.

COORDINATION: To begin the stroke cycle, press your arms downward from the overhead starting glide position. Follow this with the kick and then the arm recovery back to the original starting or glide position. Before beginning the next stroke cycle, pause and stretch your body during your glide. The useful cues for the coordination of the inverted breaststroke are: arms, legs, recover, glide.

The Windmill Backstroke

The windmill backstroke differs from the other backstroke arm motions in that you alternate your arms. In addition, the recovery is out of the water.

ARMS: As with the crawl stroke, each arm rotates alternately from the shoulder, with one pulling underwater while the other returns to the starting position upward and out of the water. You can try the S-pull variation by bending your arms slightly as you pull.

To begin the recovery, lift one arm straight up and overhead near the midline of your body. Then move your hand back with your pinky down under the water for the catch. For the pull, bring your arm in back of you in a semicircle. As your thumb touches your outer thigh, rotate your hand so that your little finger starts the recovery.

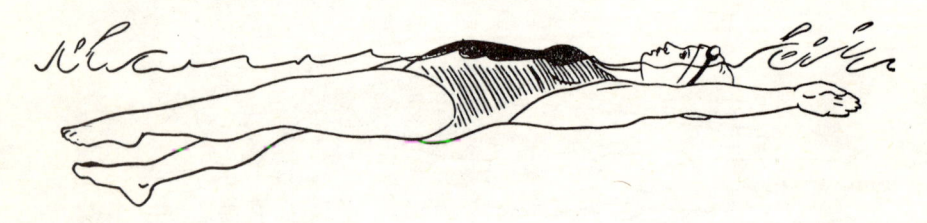

Windmill backstroke. Starting position: One arm above head, one arm at side.

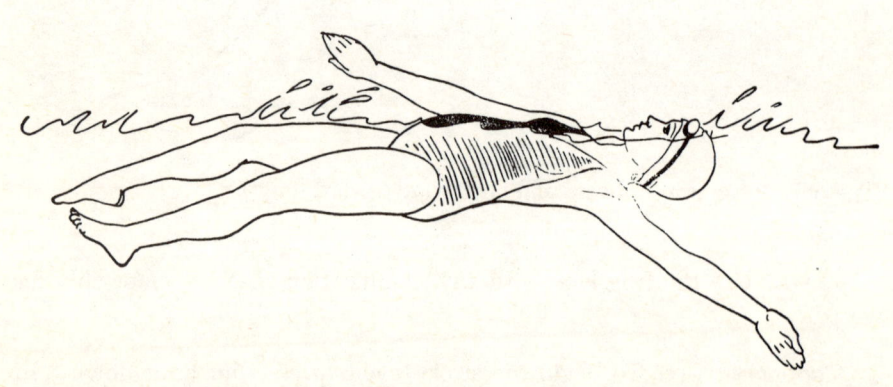

The pull: As arm above head pulls down into water, arm at side lifts out of water.

BACKSTROKE 35

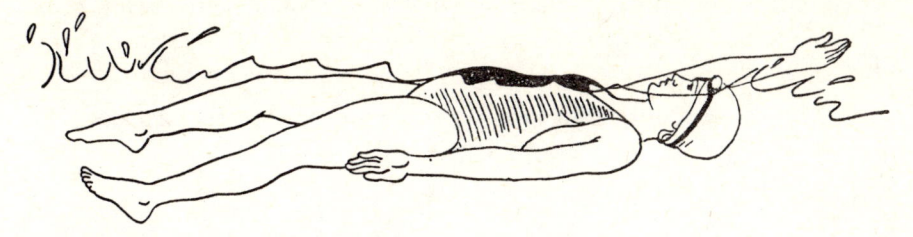

Alternate and rotate arms from the shoulder, using flutter kick.

THE S-PULL VARIATION: For a variation and more efficient backstroke propulsion, bend your arms midway through the pull. In this "bent-arm" pull, your arms rotate downward more from the shoulder. When your arm bends at the elbow while under the water at shoulder level, your hand presses more water toward your feet. (The motion is similar to throwing a ball.)

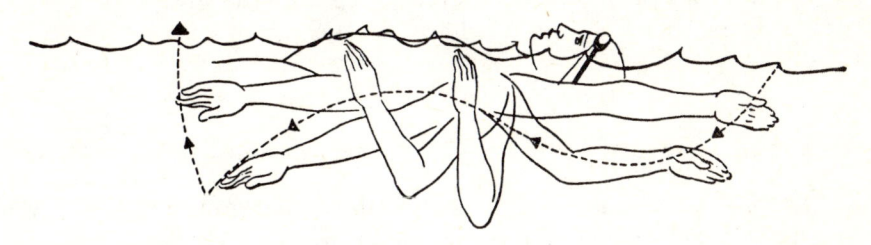

S-pull variation for windmill backstroke.

LEGS AND COORDINATION: Use a continuous flutter kick with your windmill backstroke. Your knees bend slightly as your legs alternately kick toward the surface. Keep your feet and ankles relaxed.

Special Backstroke Arm Exercises
for Use During and After Your Pregnancy

During most of your pregnancy, you will be carrying some additional weight, which can, at times, put a strain on your upper and lower back areas. The windmill, the inverted breaststroke, and the elementary backstroke arm motions can develop the muscles in these areas, which will help alleviate any discomfort. One of the areas of tension during labor and delivery is the upper shoulder area. These exercises will build up and tone this area.

TREADING:

Coordinate your sculling arm motions with your breaststroke kick.

POP-UP:

Standing in chin-deep water, try your elementary backstroke arm motion—begin with your arms on the water's surface and bring them straight down, trying to keep your balance as you pop-up. (You can also do this like a "jumping jack" exercise.)

STRETCH FOR RECOVERY TO A STANDING POSITION:

To help increase your arm flexibility, practice recovering to a stand from your back float position. To stretch, begin the downward press with arms fully extended overhead while you tuck your head toward your knees.

WINDMILL CATCH-UP:

Begin in a standing position with both of your arms in front of you with your thumbs down: rotate your right arm in a complete backward circle to its original position; then rotate the left arm in a similar manner. Then try the windmill catch-up while you're swimming.

Special Backstroke Leg Exercises for Use During and After Your Pregnancy

These exercises help to strengthen your lower abdominal muscles and develop greater tone, which will alleviate some of the pressure in that area that you may feel during your pregnancy.

SIT AND KICK:

Practice your frog and/or flutter kicking while sitting on the edge of the pool with your lower legs underwater. Balance your weight with your hands on the deck.

WALL KICK:

Hold on to the wall in the bracket position while floating on your back and practice your back flutter and breaststroke kicks.

FREE KICKING:

Practice your backstroke flutter kicking with and without fins. You may keep your arms near your sides for balance and for comfort.

ALTERNATING KICKS:

Combine both frog and flutter kicks in a sequential pattern such as ten flutter kicks followed by five frog kicks.

Special Backstroke Breathing Exercises for Use During and After Your Pregnancy

You may be considering taking a childbirth class or you may currently be enrolled in one. The Lamaze breathing techniques, frequently used in these classes, can be practiced while swimming on your back.

RAPID CHEST BREATHING: The shallow breaths that are used during the active stages of labor can be employed while sculling and/or doing the windmill backstroke.

TRANSITION BREATHING: This type of breathing is used just before you give birth and can be practiced in coordination with the arm motions of the elementary backstroke and the inverted breaststroke. Four to six pants are done as the arms bend to recover, and a large blow is done as the arms extend to the pull.

Backstroke Tips and Special Benefits for Use During and After Your Pregnancy

1. Your face can stay dry and breathing is easier.
2. You'll give your eyes a rest from wearing goggles.
3. Your backstroke arm motions are a great way to tone and strengthen your upper arms. Pushing when giving birth takes a good deal of arm strength.

4. The leg motions for the backstroke can be used interchangeably. They are also great leg toners, especially for the inner and outer thighs, the calves, and the buttocks.

5. Vertical treading may be alternated with sculling in a backstroke position. Treading water is a combination of a figure eight sculling arm motion and a breaststroke kick in a vertical position. Practice your treading in place, especially if the pool is crowded.

6. Backstroke skills afford greater comfort in the lower back area.

7. When swimming the inverted breaststroke or windmill backstroke, try your bent-arm pull (S-pull variation).

8. In the windmill backstroke, if you rotate your upper body toward your pulling arm, it will help to prevent your hips from swaying, and it adds more torso toning—another plus for labor and delivery.

9. When doing the breaststroke kick, as your buoyancy increases, remember to bend your knees as you flex your feet, dropping your heels toward the bottom of the pool. This motion comes naturally after the first few tries.

10. Swimming on your back can be a relaxed and effective means of propulsion, especially since your body's buoyancy has increased. Also, breathing is easier.

11. Be careful of other swimmers as well as that moving wall! Check at periodic intervals to see how far away you are!

7

Sidestroke

The sidestroke, with its many variations described below, is an excellent stroke that can be used during your entire pregnancy. The sidestroke is a combination of the breaststroke and the elementary backstroke. Like these strokes, the sidestroke has a long glide underwater and a similar leg motion, making it a graceful and restful stroke, especially during the later stages of your pregnancy. In addition, your face remains above water, helping your visibility and breathing.

A unique feature of the sidestroke is its eight variations: there are two scissors kicks, regular and inverted, and two arm motions, regular and top arm (overarm). These arm and leg motions can be done on either side for a total of eight variations. You will probably have a favorite combination, but give the others the old college try!

Body Position

To begin, your body should be floating on either side in a horizontal position. Your cheek is on the water so that your mouth is out of the water, and you are able to breathe continuously. Your body simulates an accordion's movement: it begins in a streamlined position, approaches a tuck position, and ends with a stretched out position once again.

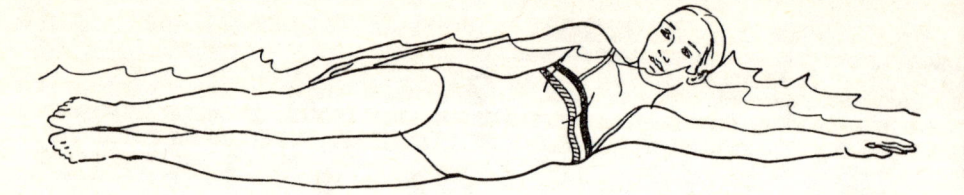

Sidestroke: Starting position.

Breathing

Try to look slightly forward so that you can keep a better eye on the pool traffic. Although your head remains out of the water, your breathing will be rhythmic. You should inhale as your body tucks and you should exhale as you glide.

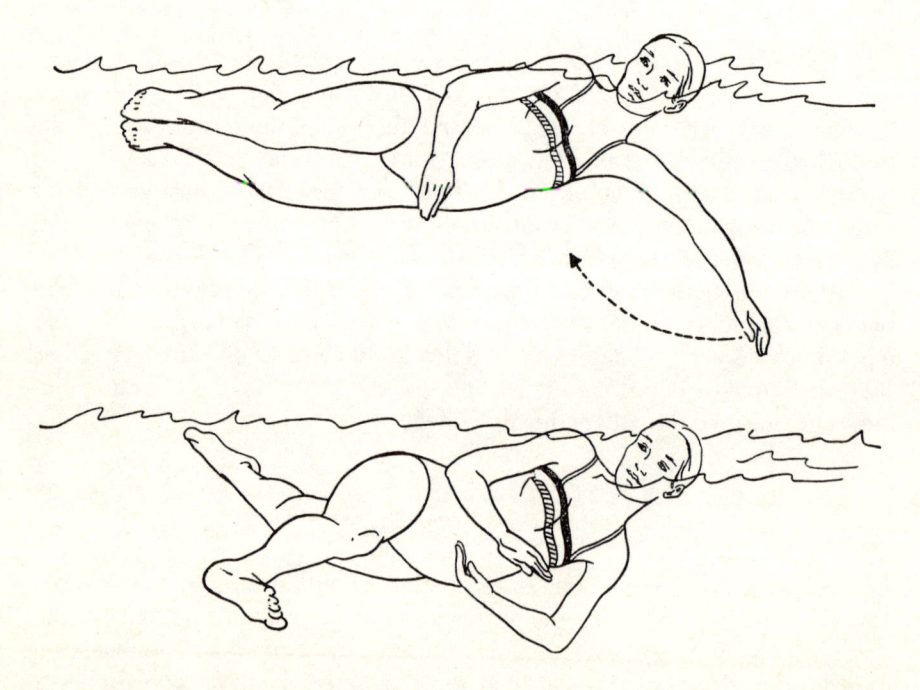

The catch and pull: Bottom arm bends at elbow, then bring arm to chest while separating legs.

Arm Motion

Your starting position begins at the glide. Your lower or bottom arm is extended overhead, in line with your body. Your upper or top arm rests along your upper side with your hand on your thigh.

For the regular sidestroke, begin the catch with your lower (bottom) arm by bending your elbow. Then push the water back toward your feet until your hand is at chest level. To recover, bring your elbow close to your side. Then extend your arm over your head, back to the starting or glide position.

Simultaneously, your upper (top) arm *recovers* by sliding the hand toward your chest. The *catch* begins with your palm facing your legs. It then pushes the water toward your feet. When your arm is completely extended, place it at your thigh and hold it there during your streamlined glide position.

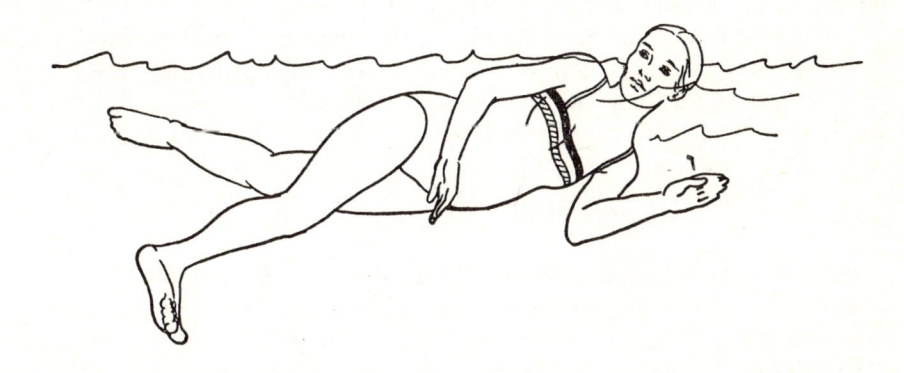

The recovery: Bring elbow of bottom arm close to side, then extend arm overhead. Bring legs together.

Remember, as one arm pulls, the other arm recovers, but both arms remain underwater throughout.

In both the regular sidestroke and top arm variation, your arms alternately pull and recover. As the top arm (closest to the water's surface) recovers, the bottom or deeper arm pulls, and vice versa. As with all other arm strokes, each sidestroke arm motion has a catch, a push, and a recovery.

TOP ARM RECOVERY VARIATION:

Here the top arm recovers in a manner similar to the crawl stroke's high elbow recovery out of the water.

Leg Motion

The sidestroke leg motion is called the scissors kick. The legs separate and then come together like a pair of scissor blades. Start in the glide position on your side with your legs extended and your toes pointed. Bring your knees toward your abdomen, approaching a 90° angle between your body and thighs. Your feet should be flexed. Your legs separate with the top leg staying forward and the bottom leg moving backward to form a V. Keep your top foot flexed and point your bottom foot as you extend your legs to a wider V position. For propulsion, squeeze your legs together while you're pointing both your feet. Now you have returned to your streamlined glide position.

Since you have been swimming with your best foot forward, be trendy and try this for a kick! Begin your scissors kick as before, but move your bottom leg forward and your top leg backward.

Coordinating Arms and Legs

The stroke can be coordinated by relating it to a contraction or to a wave-type motion. From your extended glide position, the first part of the stroke is bringing both your arms and your legs together to a tuck or fetal-like position. This is the height or peak of your contraction. The second part of your stroke occurs when both the arms and legs extend back to the end of the wave or to the streamlined position.

Special Sidestroke Arm Exercises for Use During and After Your Pregnancy

UNDER AND OVERS:

Alternately change from the regular arm stroke to the overarm stroke in a pattern such as two overarm and then two regular strokes, and repeat. Practice on both sides. During pushing, your arms get a good workout—strengthen them now.

COMBO PULL:

For variety, begin with two strokes of inverted breaststroke; then roll to either side during the glide and continue with two sidestroke arm motions. Continue alternating to both left and right sides.

Special Sidestroke Leg Exercises for Use During and After Your Pregnancy

BICYCLE PEDAL:

Practice a bicycle-pedaling leg motion—you can do this during your warm-up or stretch-out while sitting on the deck with your legs dangling in the water, or any time during your workout in chest-deep water. This pedaling motion is used as a leg motion in treading.

WALL KICKING:

Hold on to the wall in your bracket position and try the four different variations of the scissors kick.

KICKBOARD KICK:

Hold the kickboard at waist level with your top arm and practice the four kick variations. Use your bottom arm for stability.

TRUDGEN KICK:

Alternate the scissors kick with a few (about four) flutter kicks. You can also do this with your crawl stroke arm motion.

All the above exercises help develop your leg muscles, which will be helpful during labor and delivery.

Special Sidestroke Breathing Exercises for Use During and After Your Pregnancy

The sidestroke is an excellent and relaxing stroke with which to practice your "cleansing breath." You may be familiar with this breathing technique from your childbirth preparation classes. Inhale fully and exhale slowly and completely. Coordinate inhaling with the first part of the sidestroke. Commence exhaling at the tuck position, and then exhale continuously through your *glide*. This will help you get extra oxygen.

Combination Stroke (The Trudgen)

The trudgen crawl is a combination of the crawl stroke breathing and arm motions with a narrow scissors kick on the breathing side. It can be an effective yet comfortable variation of these strokes, especially if you find your legs tiring when you flutter kick.

Medley of Strokes

It is said that variety is the spice of life, so the medley stroke combinations are provided to add that needed spice. Vary the number of strokes you take for the following:

- Crawl—windmill backstroke—crawl
- Elementary backstroke—sidestroke—breaststroke—sidestroke—inverted breaststroke
- Try your own variations.

Sidestroke Tips and Special Benefits for Use During and After Your Pregnancy

1. Since you can look in the direction you are swimming, you do not have to be overly concerned about colliding with other swimmers. Remember to look, listen, and stay to the right in your lane.
2. The sidestroke helps to stretch, condition, and develop the muscles on your sides and torso.
3. Try all eight variations of the sidestroke.
4. Using the high elbow recovery of the top arm variation will provide you with more balance as your pregnancy advances. (This is also a plus for your high elbow crawl stroke recovery.)
5. For conditioning, flexibility, tone, and strength of your inner thigh muscles, the scissors kick and its four variations are great.
6. The sidestroke's tuck body position helps to relieve lower back pain, which you may experience from time to time during your pregnancy.

SIDESTROKE   45

7. You can breathe easily doing the sidestroke because your face is out of the water.

8. The special qualities of the sidestroke are its streamlined motion and its slow and relaxing style.

9. The scissors kick, regular and inverted, can be used for the trudgen crawl stroke variation.

10. The trudgen crawl can be a comfortable stroke during your third trimester (crawl arm motion with scissors kick).

The chart on the following page will serve to provide you with a ready and handy reference guide for "stroke cues."

Stroke Cues Chart

STROKE CUES

Stroke	Body Position & Breathing	Arm Movement	Leg Movement	Coordination
Crawl (Freestyle)	Prone (face down) Rhythmic breathing (head turns to one side)	Alternating hand-over-hand—S-pull	Flutter Kick	One breath per arm cycle Any number of flutter kicks (Usually 4-6 per arm cycle)
Breaststroke	Prone Head lifts for inhalation	Heart-shaped pull	Frog Kick	Pull (and inhale)-Kick-Glide
Backstroke • Sculling	Supine (face-up) Breathe normally	Figure Eight	Flutter Kick	Smooth propulsive movement of body
• Elementary	Supine (face up) Breathe normally	Bend-Extend-Press & Glide	Frog Kick (on back)	Simultaneous movement of arms & legs: Up (inhale)-Out-Together (exhale) & Glide
• Inverted Breaststroke	Supine (arms begin overhead)	Pull from overhead position to side	Frog Kick (on back)	Pull-Kick-Recover & Glide
• Windmill Backstroke	Supine	Alternating straight arm recovery—Bent arm S-pull Variation	Flutter Kick (on back)	Simultaneous and continuous movement of arms and legs
Sidestroke	On either side (lower arm extended) Head at water level	Alternating underwater pull (top-arm-out-of-water recovery)	Scissors and/or inverted scissors kick	Glide-Part 1-Tuck-Part 2-Glide

9

Push-offs and Turns

Push-offs

During your pregnancy, there is one basic way to begin your swim; it is called the in-the-water push-off. Entries into the water from the deck, diving and jumping, are not recommended during your pregnancy.

CRAWL STROKE AND BREASTSTROKE PUSH-OFF:

Stand in the water with your knees slightly bent, your back foot against the wall, your arms extended in front of you in the glide position. Lower your body underwater and place your other foot against the wall and push with both legs into a glide. Begin swimming when your glide begins to lose momentum.

BACKSTROKE BEGINNINGS:

Face the wall and hold on with both hands; your elbows should be slightly bent. Place both feet comfortably against the wall below the water's surface. Bring your body into a slightly tucked position by bending your elbows a little more. To begin, gently swing your arms to an over-the-head position; as you extend on your back, try to keep your hips close to the water's surface as you push off with your legs and glide.

Backstroke starting position.

SIDESTROKE PUSH-OFF:

Stand sideways to the pool wall and hold the wall with your inside hand with your arm bent at the elbow, then extend your other arm forward in the direction you will be swimming. Remember to rest your cheek on the water's surface before pushing off so that your body will be in the proper alignment.

SPECIAL PUSH-OFF TIPS
FOR USE DURING AND AFTER YOUR PREGNANCY:

1. Use the resistance of the pool wall or bottom to help give you an efficient push-off.
2. Your legs provide the power for the push-off; the effort of pushing off will help to strengthen and condition them.
3. Before you start to swim, your head should be aligned with your body. Your arms should be overhead covering your ears during the glide and your body should be streamlined and stretched out.
4. As your pregnancy advances, you will become more buoyant. To help counterbalance/counteract the tendency to "pop-up" in the water during your crawl push-off, you should lower your head and angle your arms under the water toward the bottom of the pool.
5. In your breaststroke, try to push off at a downward angle toward

the pool's bottom with your hips higher than your head and arms—you'll feel as if you're going downhill for a moment. (This is known as downstreaming and will give you more glide.)

6. The longer you hold your streamlined glide position during your push-off, the more it will help stretch and condition your legs.

7. In your backstroke push-off, try to tilt your head slightly backward—this will help to arch your back.

8. You can use the sidestroke push-off as a variation of the crawl starting position. This may be more comfortable for you as your pregnancy progresses.

9. Always push off gently.

Turns

Now that we've described push-offs, you should know what to do when you reach the other end of the pool. This section of the book explains how to turn your body in a graceful and efficient manner. The object of a turn is to use your body's momentum to make a 180° rotation. During your pregnancy, I recommend that you use the turning style known as the "open turn." This is the only type of turn which will be discussed.

THE CRAWL STROKE AND BREASTSTROKE TURN:

For the crawl stroke turn, swim to the wall with both eyes open, looking slightly forward so you can see a marker or the wall. When you are about one body length from the wall, complete your arm stroke, kick in with one arm extended and turn your other arm in the direction in which you will be turning. As your forward hand touches the wall, bend your elbow to bring your body close to the wall, keeping your head out of the water. Bend your knees under your body and turn away from your forward hand. As you rotate, place your feet on the wall, stretch out your arms in the direction in which you are going to swim. You are ready for the push-off.

For the breaststroke turn, touch the pool edge with both hands and turn in either direction, then release the wall with either arm, and push-off.

THE BACKSTROKE TURN:

No matter which backstroke arm motion you are using, the movement for this turn will be the same. As you reach the wall, extend one hand overhead and grasp the pool's edge. Turn 180° in the direction of your contact arm, bending and lifting your knees as you turn toward the contact arm. Keep your free arm extended on the surface of the water. Place your feet comfortably on the wall for your push-off. You should be facing the wall as you push off. As you push off, extend both arms overhead for streamlined position.

THE SIDESTROKE TURN:

There are two ways to turn while swimming the sidestroke. The first way is used if you only swim on one side. To do this turn you touch the wall with your extended arm, and then you tuck your knees slightly toward your chest as you bring the other arm to the wall (as in the breaststroke turn). Complete the turn by releasing your forward arm from the wall. Finish with your push-off; you will face the opposite side of the pool. The second way to turn is for the versatile sidestroker who can swim on either side. Begin by touching the wall with the extended arm. As you tuck your knees and place your feet on the wall, facing in the same direction, complete the turn by using your sidestroke push-off.

SPECIAL TURNING TIPS FOR USE DURING AND AFTER YOUR PREGNANCY:

1. Streamline and stretch your body out as you glide after the push-off.
2. For all turns, use your free arm to help you turn by using a small sculling motion.
3. Both your abdominal muscles and legs are used during turns. This will develop strength you will need later on.
4. Your ability to judge the distance between your body and the end of the pool as you approach the wall will improve with practice so that you will be able to assume the proper position to turn.
5. When swimming backstroke, use a pool guide such as a ladder, light window, flag, or chair to help you glide into the wall. Remember to turn in the same direction as your contact arm.
6. During your breaststroke turn, remember to turn in the direction of the extended arm.
7. Try both sidestroke turns. Be versatile and try all eight variations of the sidestroke.
8. When using a kickboard, reach for the wall with one hand while

the other hand holds on to the kickboard. Turn 180° (toward the kickboard) and continue as in the open turn.

9. When using fins, flex your feet toward your shins with the fins touching the wall as flat as possible—this will prevent you from tripping on them.

II

Waterworks Exercises

10

Introduction to Waterworks

Waterworks is an exercise program specifically designed to be performed in the water. These exercises can be of tremendous benefit to you during your pregnancy. Each exercise will help to trim, strengthen, firm, and stretch the muscles involved in childbirth, and the exercises are targeted at particularly troublesome body areas. Use common sense in choosing the exercises you do, and have a wonderful time with your Waterworks.

For each exercise, I will describe:

- the benefits derived from the exercise,
- the starting position for the exercise,
- how to do the exercise, and
- extra tips for technique, variations, repetitions, and duration.

As your pregnancy progresses, you'll become more buoyant, and the Waterworks exercises are designed to take advantage of this buoyancy. You will find that the Waterworks exercises are fun and relaxing, as well as very beneficial. So get your suit on, gear up, and take the plunge!

Using Waterworks

You should incorporate Waterworks exercises into your warm-up and stretch-out for each swim session. Select exercises appropriate to your fitness level and stage of pregnancy. Be sure to vary your exercises so that you regularly perform exercises from each of the five categories of Waterworks. The five categories are:

- Breathing Exercises
- Upper Body Exercises
- Middle Body Exercises
- Lower Body Exercises
- Total Body Exercises

Bonus Benefits of Waterworks

Waterworks will not only help get and keep you fit, they offer you these extra benefits:

- You can easily select exercises that are appropriate to the stage of your pregnancy.
- You can do Waterworks when the pool is too crowded for swimming, or when you are too tired for comfortable swimming.
- You can keep your hair dry while doing them.
- They are comfortable and specially designed to employ your increasing buoyancy, e.g., floating will relax you.
- You can do and enjoy these exercises regardless of your ability to swim.
- You can readily adjust the number of repetitions or duration of each exercise to the stage of your pregnancy, your fitness level, and your daily comfort.
- Waterworks have been designed to work different parts of the body.
- You can use Waterworks during your postpartum period for your warm-up and stretch-out.

General Waterworks Tips

- Exercise only as much as is comfortable; rest when you are tired and avoid straining.
- Perform each repetition of an exercise in a slow and steady fashion—imagine you're performing a form of yoga. Concentrate on every movement and feel your body as it performs. Avoid pumping or jerky movements.
- Unless you are accustomed to vigorous exercise, start your program using five exercises, one from each of the exercise categories.
- Breathe deeply, rhythmically, and continuously throughout each exer-

cise; deep breathing will enhance the pleasure and relaxation of the exercises. (Be careful not to hyperventilate).
- Begin and end each Waterworks exercise with a cleansing breath.* (This will help to train you to use the cleansing breath during labor and delivery.)
- If at any time you feel a strain, stop; if any discomfort persists, check with your doctor.
- Add effleurage (a light, gentle, fingertip massage of the abdomen) whenever possible, so that it will come naturally when you need it during labor and delivery.
- Try to complement every swim session with the Waterworks exercises that are appropriate to your stage of pregnancy.
- Exercise to music whenever possible.
- Do not jump, dive, or use any strenuous wall push-off.
- Be creative—combine exercises and design your sequence and variations to fit your needs.

Waterworks and Prepared Childbirth

Waterworks exercises will complement childbirth preparation by helping to make you stronger, more fit, and more limber. The exercises will give you practice in employing the cleansing breath and effleurage, and will teach you how to concentrate on your body's movements and how to relax!

At-Home Waterworks

At the end of this section, "at-home" Waterworks are described, which you can do on the days you can't get to the pool.

ABOVE ALL, WHEN DOING YOUR WATERWORKS EXERCISES, RELAX, BREATHE DEEPLY, AND ENJOY YOURSELF!

* A cleansing breath is a very slow, deep inhalation through the nose and a slow exhalation through the mouth. Its purpose is to help produce total relaxation at the beginning and at the end of each exercise (or contraction during labor).

11

Breathing Waterworks

EXERCISE: *Cleansing Breath Breathing*
BENEFITS: Develops the ability to breathe deeply and fully to achieve more complete air exchange. The "cleansing breath" is used during labor and delivery.
STARTING POSITION: Stand in the pool in waist-deep water with your arms extended out to the sides.
HOW TO DO IT: Inhale deeply and slowly through your nose, then exhale slowly and completely through your mouth. Do 5 repetitions, rest, and repeat.
EXTRA TIPS: Try this variation:
- Stand in chest-deep water, holding on to the pool wall with one hand and bending your knees so that your face is just above the surface. Inhale through your nose, then put your face into the water and exhale simultaneously through your nose and mouth. Repeat.
- The cleansing breath exercises should be done before and after every warm-up and stretch-out exercise. Since breathing is so important for your comfort in the water, these exercises are a great way to practice coordination, as well as to warm up the muscles.

EXERCISE: *Breathe and Reach*
BENEFITS: Combines the cleansing breath with an arm reach, increasing your air exchange and oxygen absorption. It also helps to expand lung capacity and provides the baby with more oxygen.

STARTING POSITION: Stand in waist-deep water with your arms extended to the sides.

HOW TO DO IT: Lift your arms to an overhead position as you inhale. Then slowly return your arms to the starting position as you exhale. Start with 5 repetitions and work your way up to as many repetitions as is comfortable.

EXTRA TIPS: Try these variations:
- As your arms are extended overhead, stretch them upward alternately a few times. What a great stretch!
- During the early stages of your pregnancy, you may cross your arms in front of you as you inhale and raise your arms overhead as you exhale.

EXERCISE: *Breathing with Head Circles*

BENEFITS: Tones and stretches the muscles in the head and neck areas. Develops the ability to detect and control tension (which often manifests itself first in muscle tension in the head and neck areas). This will also help you to relax during labor and delivery.

STARTING POSITION: Stand in neck-deep water with your head forward.

HOW TO DO IT: Rotate your head in one direction, inhaling deeply through your nose and mouth until your head has completed half a circle (your head will be back at this point). Then exhale through your nose and mouth as your head completes the circle to its original position. Start with 5 repetitions, and work your way up to as many repetitions as is comfortable. Repeat the exercise, moving your head in the other direction.

EXTRA TIPS:
- For variety, and to achieve maximum flexibility, alternate counterclockwise and clockwise head circles.
- Add your cleansing breath to your head circles by inhaling through your nose and exhaling through your mouth.

EXERCISE: *Breathing and Bobbing*

BENEFITS: Develops your general breathing technique and increases breath control.

STARTING POSITION: Stand in chest-deep water.

HOW TO DO IT: Inhale deeply through your nose and mouth, then exhale slowly and completely through your nose and mouth. Repeat 5 times. Then combine this breathing technique with bobbing. Inhale just before bending your knees to submerge. Exhale continuously through your nose and mouth underwater. Then, still exhaling, straighten your knees to emerge from the water. Repeat.

EXTRA TIPS:
- Practice controlled breathing by deliberately timing your exhalations to take more time than your inhalations. Avoid holding your breath.
- You may wish to hold on to the pool wall or ladder while you're standing or bobbing.
- You can supplement your breathing exercises by performing crawl and breaststroke arm motions while breathing.

EXERCISE: *Rhythmic Breathing*
BENEFITS: Develops breath control and the ability to relax, as well as providing the mother and unborn baby with maximum quantities of oxygen. It is also a necessary skill for the crawl stroke.
STARTING POSITION: Stand in chest-deep water. Bend at the knees and waist so that your face is just above the surface of the water.
HOW TO DO IT: Inhale through your nose and mouth, then place your face in the water and exhale through your nose and mouth continuously. Turn your face to the right so that your nose and mouth just clear the water, and inhale deeply through your nose and mouth. Turn your face back into the water and exhale. Repeat 5 to 10 times, rest, and then repeat the exercise turning your face to the left to breathe.
EXTRA TIPS:
- You can practice your crawl stroke with this exercise by adding the arm stroke to your breathing. Practice by standing and then walking forward as you stroke and breathe. Remember that as one hand extends forward to stroke and the other recovers, you turn your face to the side of the recovering hand to breathe.
- Try alternate breathing; this is similar to the technique of rhythmic breathing except you turn your face to breathe only once for every 3 arm strokes. This means that your head will turn to breathe to one side and 3 arm strokes later you will turn your head to the other side to breathe. Alternate breathing is not only a terrific breathing exercise; it also stretches and tones the muscles of the head and neck.
- You can practice your crawl stroke with alternate breathing just as you do with rhythmic breathing, except that you breathe on every third stroke, and turn your face alternately to the right and the left. Remember, turn your face toward the recovering arm and away from the extended arm.

EXERCISE: *Four Breathing Patterns Used During Labor and Delivery*
BENEFITS: Develops the breathing techniques you will use during labor and delivery, and increases breath control.

BREATHING WATERWORKS

STARTING POSITION: Stand in chest-deep water.
HOW TO DO IT:
- To practice for breathing during the *early stages of labor,* breathe using slow chest breathing (deep, full chest expansions) at a rate of 6 to 9 breaths per minute. Do this for 1 minute.
- To practice for *breathing during transition,* combine panting breaths (short, shallow breaths) with a deep, full exhalation (a "blow"); do 4 to 6 pants, then a blow. Repeat for 1½ minutes.
- To practice for *pushing* and birth, use a sequence of 2 quick cleansing breaths, followed by a deep inhalation through the nose held 5 to 10 seconds before a deep exhalation through the mouth. Repeat for 1½ minutes. Push down gently—do this with your coach rather than alone.

EXTRA TIPS:
- Remember to begin and end each breathing exercise with a cleansing breath.
- Combine your effleurage with your breathing.
- Try to concentrate on a point during your breathing practice.
- The accompanying chart will remind you of the breathing patterns you will use during labor and delivery.
- The breathing pattern used during the early stages of labor can be practiced while you are swimming the catch-up crawl stroke, sidestroke, or breaststroke.
- The breathing pattern used during active labor can be practiced intermittently while swimming, at the beginning, middle, and end of laps. It can also be used while sculling or doing the elementary backstroke.
- The breathing pattern used during transition can be practiced while doing the breaststroke, inverted breaststroke, or sidestroke.

BREATHING PATTERNS USED DURING LABOR AND DELIVERY

Stage of Labor	Approximate Time	Frequency of Contractions	Duration of Contractions	Intensity of Contractions	Dilation	Type of Breathing Used
1st- Early	8-10 hours	20 mins.	30-45 secs.	Mild to Moderate	0-4 cm.	6-9 breaths per minute (slow chest)
Active	4-5 hours	2-3 mins.	45 secs.-1 min.	Moderate to Intense	4-8 cm.	Rapid/shallow chest (pants-he-he)
Transition	½ hour-	1-1½ mins.	1-2 mins.	Intense	8-10 cm.	Rapid chest and blow (4-6 pants & blow)
2nd-Pushing & to Birth	Minutes to an Hour	2-3 mins.	1-1½ mins.	Intense	10 cm.	2 quick cleansing breaths; on 3rd, hold and push—breathe in and repeat (Deep inhalation, approximately 5-10 seconds of holding; push down and out—release & repeat)
3rd- Afterbirth	5-30 mins.	2-3 mins.	1-1½ mins.	Moderate	10 cm.	Same as the pushing techniques and relaxation techniques

12

Upper Body Waterworks

EXERCISE: *Medley of Pulls* (Arm Strokes)

BENEFITS: Tones and strengthens all upper body muscles. Reviews major swim strokes. Arm strength is important since you will rely on your arms for support in pushing.

STARTING POSITION: Stand in chest-deep water.

HOW TO DO IT: Do 10 arm strokes for each of the following:
- Crawl stroke (10 strokes with each arm)
- Breaststroke
- Sidestroke
- Backstroke (10 strokes with each arm)
- Your choice of strokes

EXTRA TIPS:
- Balance your body by placing one foot ahead of the other.
- Alternate stroke speeds (e.g., do 5 easy strokes followed by 5 vigorous strokes).
- Create your own sequence of arm strokes.
- Practice rhythmic and/or alternate breathing with the crawl arm motion.
- Choose strokes you know or would like to practice.
- Hand paddles may be used for added resistance.

EXERCISE: *Arm Presses/Front to Back Water Push*

BENEFITS: Tones and strengthens upper body muscles; this is important because strengthened chest muscles will help to support your breasts as they swell. This exercise also promotes upper body flexibility and helps you to identify and control upper body tension.

STARTING POSITION: Stand in neck-deep water.

HOW TO DO IT: There are two methods:

- Extend your right arm in front of you at shoulder height with your palm facing down. Extend your left arm behind you at shoulder height with your palm facing down. Press both of your hands down toward your thighs and then upward in an arc so that you finish with the right arm extended behind you and your left arm extended in front of you. Turn your palms so that they face down and repeat. Start with 10 repetitions and work up to as many as you can do comfortably.
- Extend both of your arms in front of you at shoulder height with your palms facing outward. Press your arms away from each other until they are extended out to your sides. Then turn your hands over and press your arms together until your palms meet. Start with 10 repetitions.

EXTRA TIPS:

- For both exercises, add your cleansing breath: breathe in through your nose and out through your mouth on succeeding arm presses.
- Keep your feet spread apart and your knees slightly bent to help you maintain your balance. To increase the difficulty of the exercise, use hand paddles.
- Perform all movements slowly and deliberately.
- For variety you may combine one or both of the exercises with knee bends.

EXERCISE: *Arm Circles*

BENEFITS: Develops shoulder, arm, and upper back strength, which will be of great benefit when you support yourself during labor and pushing.

STARTING POSITION: Stand in neck-deep water with your feet shoulder width apart and your knees slightly bent.

HOW TO DO IT: Extend and straighten your arms to the side at shoulder height just under the surface of the water. Rotate your arms forward in a small circle. Start with 5 repetitions and work up to a comfortable number of repetitions. Repeat the exercise, rotating your arms backward in a small circle. Then repeat both the forward and backward circles, but make bigger circles with your arms.

EXTRA TIPS:

- To increase resistance, use hand paddles while doing the exercise with small circles.
- Try this variation: place your hands on your shoulders and rotate your arms at the shoulders moving your arms in a circle. (Chicken wings!)
- Arm circles is a great warm-up exercise for the crawl stroke!

UPPER BODY WATERWORKS

EXERCISE: *Arm Works/Swim Salute*

BENEFITS: Tones and strengthens the upper body muscles to give you the strength and flexibility you will need during labor and delivery. These exercises will help you relax and get the "kinks" out. The baby will love them too!

STARTING POSITION: Stand in chest-deep water.

HOW TO DO IT:

- Lift your arms overhead and stretch upward with your palms clasped together. Then release your hands and stretch each arm overhead independently.
- Grasp each elbow with the opposite hand and stretch. Twist your torso to the right keeping your feet motionless and pulling on your left elbow with your right hand. Then twist to the left pulling on your right elbow with your left hand. Repeat.

EXTRA TIPS:

- Extend your arms in front of you at shoulder height and clasp your palms. Twist your torso to the right, keeping your feet motionless and pulling on your left hand with your right hand. Then twist to the left pulling on your right hand with your left. Repeat. Anchors aweigh!
- Breathe deeply and continuously as you do these arm works.

EXERCISE: *Hang Ten*

BENEFITS: Stretches and relaxes the upper body. Neck tension can be identified and eliminated.

STARTING POSITION: Stand and place your back against the pool wall. Reach over your shoulders and grasp the pool edge (or a ladder) with your hands shoulder-width apart.

HOW TO DO IT: Bend your knees so that your feet lift from the bottom, allowing the weight of your body to stretch your arms and upper body.

EXTRA TIPS:

- Relax your head and neck muscles and breathe deeply as you stretch.
- To increase the stretch, move your hands closer together.

EXERCISE: *Sculling*

BENEFITS: Sculling helps to ease neck tension. Gently tones the upper body muscles, especially those of the chest that help support breasts. Sculling is a basic skill used in synchronized swimming.

STARTING POSITION: Stand in shoulder-deep water with your arms extended forward and under the surface close to each other, your palms facing together, your hands arched slightly, and your fingers pointed upward.

Hang Ten starting position.

HOW TO DO IT: Move your hands in a figure eight motion, keeping your upper arms relatively motionless. To do this, turn your palms downward and outward and press your hands out past shoulder width, then turn your palms inward and press your hands in until they are two inches apart; then turn your palms outward and repeat the movement. Breathe slowly in and out through your nose and mouth as you scull.

EXTRA TIPS:
• Float on your back and support yourself in the water using just the sculling movement, bringing your hands down to your sides, next to your hips.
• You can do different sculling motions (for synchronized swimming) by changing the angle or pitch of your hands.

EXERCISE: *Wall Push-Ups*
BENEFITS: Strengthens the shoulders, arms, and chest muscles to give you strength you will need during pushing for delivery. Stronger chest muscles will help to support your breasts.
STARTING POSITION: Stand in chest-deep water facing the pool wall. Your feet should be far enough away from the wall so that you can just reach the pool edge. Grasp the pool edge with your hands shoulder width apart.

UPPER BODY WATERWORKS

HOW TO DO IT:

- Slowly bend your elbows, keeping your body straight and your feet stationary until your chin approaches the pool edge. Then slowly straighten your arms until you resume a standing position. Inhale through your nose as you bend your elbows, and exhale through your mouth as you straighten your arms. Bend and straighten your arms slowly. Start with 5 repetitions and work up to a comfortable number.
- Move closer to the pool wall until your feet just touch it. Place your hands in the pool gutter, bending your elbows and centering your weight over your hands. Bob and straighten your arms to lift yourself partially out of the water. Try to support your body with your elbows locked for a moment. Then slowly bend your elbows to lower yourself back into the water. Exhale through your mouth as you straighten your arms and inhale through your nose as you bend your elbows. All movements should be slow and continuous.

This exercise can also be used as a means of exiting the pool during your early stages of pregnancy. For help in using this exit, bounce off the bottom, giving a little push with your feet.

Push down on kickboard to strengthen upper body.

EXTRA TIPS: To begin strengthening your upper body for wall push-ups, use a kickboard for resistance, as shown in illustration.

13

Middle Body Waterworks

EXERCISE: *Circle Spray*

BENEFITS: Tones the waist and torso and develops middle body flexibility. A great way to get going!

STARTING POSITION: Stand in waist-deep water with your arms extended out to your sides and your fingers pointing downward. Spread your feet shoulder width apart.

HOW TO DO IT: Twist at the torso to the right, keeping your feet stationary and your arms straight. Your fingertips should spray the water as you move. Return to the starting position and twist to the left. Repeat. Start with 10 twists to each side.

EXTRA TIPS: To add variety, you can do this exercise while keeping your hands on your hips under the water.

EXERCISE: *Body and Hip Press*

BENEFITS: Tones the abdominal muscles, which will assist the uterus during pushing.

STARTING POSITION: Stand in waist-deep water, one side of your body against the pool wall. Grasp the pool edge with the hand closest to it. Place your other hand on your hip.

HOW TO DO IT: Press your hip against the wall and bend forward at the waist. Straighten and then repeat. Turn around and repeat the exercise on the other side. Start with 10 repetitions on each side.

MIDDLE BODY WATERWORKS

EXTRA TIPS: Try these variations:
- Reach across your body with your outside hand (the one away from the wall) and grasp the pool edge. You'll find that this is a terrific stretch.
- Add leg lifts, forward and backward, to the Body and Hip Press.

EXERCISE: *Leg Lifts*

BENEFITS: Strengthens the muscles of the abdomen and thighs and develops middle body flexibility. This will be a great aid to comfortably carrying your child during pregnancy and will help you during labor and pushing. These exercises should only be used during the early stages of your pregnancy (through the second trimester, if your doctor approves).

STARTING POSITION: Stand in waist-deep water with your back against the pool wall. Hold on to the pool edge with both hands. If you wish, you may stand in a corner of the pool.

HOW TO DO IT:
- Bring your feet together. Press the small of your back against the pool wall and lift your legs, with your knees straight, until your legs form a 90° angle with your torso. Breathe in through your nose as you raise your legs and out through your mouth as you lower your legs. Begin with 5 repetitions and work up.
- For an extra leg stretch, stand facing the wall and lift one leg to the pool edge while leaning forward over that leg. Hold the wall for support and extra stretch. Hold for thirty seconds, then change legs.

EXTRA TIPS:
- You can do these exercises while supporting yourself in the water by holding a kickboard to your chest.
- As your pregnancy advances, you may find it more comfortable to lift your legs or knees, as the case may be, to the side, rather than straight up.

EXERCISE: *Hula-Hoop Hip Rotation*

BENEFITS: Strengthens and loosens the lower back, which is very helpful for avoiding the back discomfort that frequently accompanies pregnancy.

STARTING POSITION: Stand in waist-deep water, facing the pool wall. Extend both of your arms and grasp the pool edge.

HOW TO DO IT: Bend your elbows and swing your hips to the right and then toward the wall in a circle. As your body approaches the center line of the circle, extend your belly out and arch your back slightly. Continue to circle to the left. As your body approaches its original position, bend slightly at the waist to stretch your back. Start with 10 repetitions. Then repeat the exercise circling in the opposite direction.

EXTRA TIPS:
- Exaggerate your movements to get a better stretch.
- If you push and pull vigorously on the pool edge as you swing your hips, you'll help to strengthen your arm muscles.

EXERCISE: *Modified Sit-Ups*

BENEFITS: Strengthens and tones the muscles of the abdomen and thighs.

STARTING POSITION: Float on your back in chest-deep water with your neck resting on the pool edge. Grasp the pool edge with both hands with arms extended to the sides.

HOW TO DO IT: Pull your knees to your chest. Then straighten your legs. Remember to breathe in through your nose as you draw your knees in and out through your mouth as you straighten your legs. Begin with 5 repetitions.

Modified sit-up: neck on edge of pool, pull knees toward chest.

EXTRA TIPS:
- As your pregnancy advances, you may be more comfortable bringing your knees to one side.
- This exercise can be done throughout your pregnancy and during your postpartum period, with your doctor's approval.
- Be sure not to "sit up" too far; a small movement will suffice to exercise your abdominal muscles.

MIDDLE BODY WATERWORKS

EXERCISE: *Pelvic Rock*

BENEFITS: Strengthens and stretches the muscles of the back and abdomen. This will help ease the backache you may experience during pregnancy by conditioning the muscles most stressed at this time.

STARTING POSITION: Stand in waist-deep water with your back and hips against the pool wall. Grasp the pool edge with both hands.

HOW TO DO IT: Arch your back so that your abdomen is thrust forward. Your upper back and hips should maintain contact with the pool wall. Start with 10 repetitions.

VARIATION: While keeping your upper back and hips against the pool wall, alternately raise and lower your knees toward your chest. Lift your knees only as far as is comfortable. Start with 5 repetitions with each knee.

EXTRA TIPS: These are great exercises for working out the kinks in the lower back. Breathe slowly and regularly with each repetition.

EXERCISE: *Pushing*

BENEFITS: Strengthens the abdominal, arm, and lower back muscles, all of which will be called into play as you push during delivery.

Practice pushing at pool's edge.

STARTING POSITION: For this exercise, you'll need a partner. Stand in the pool in chest-deep water, your hands at your sides, with your partner standing behind you to support you.

HOW TO DO IT: After two cleansing breaths, bend your knees and pull them upward with your arms as you hold your breath. Assume a back float position with your partner supporting you under your hips. After two cleansing breaths, bend your knees and pull them upward with your arms as you hold your breath and push down with your pelvic muscles.

EXTRA TIPS:
- If your childbirth coach is not available you can practice this exercise by standing with your side to the pool wall and holding on to the pool edge for support with one arm. Bend the knee that's away from the wall and place your free hand behind the bent knee. Practice your pushing breathing exercise as you pull your knee upward.

EXERCISE: *Back Massage*

BENEFITS: Relaxes the back muscles. A terrific way to relieve stress and ease the back strain and discomfort that may accompany pregnancy.

STARTING POSITION: Stand in chest-deep water with your partner standing behind you.

HOW TO DO IT: Your partner should gently massage your back, beneath the surface of the water, using the heels of his palms. The back massage combined with the soothing properties of the water will make you feel wonderful!

EXTRA TIPS: If you are taking a prepared childbirth class, your coach can help you with this exercise. If you don't have a partner available, reach around and massage your own back.

14

Lower Body Waterworks

EXERCISE: *Back Kicking and Relaxing*

BENEFITS: Loosens and strengthens your lower back and legs. This will ease muscle strain during pregnancy and help you support yourself and push during labor and delivery.

STARTING POSITION: Float on your back with your neck resting on the pool edge. Grasp the pool edge with both hands.

HOW TO DO IT: Flutter kick, bending your knees slightly, keeping your ankles loose, and pointing and flexing your toes as you kick. Start to kick slowly, then kick progressively faster. As you become more comfortable you may increase the duration of your kicking exercises. Concentrate on breathing deeply as you kick—breathe in through your nose and out through your mouth.

EXTRA TIPS: You may wish to alternate 5 seconds of hard with 5 seconds of easy kicking.

EXERCISE: *Medley of Kicks*

BENEFITS: Tones and strengthens muscles of the hips and legs. This will make your pregnancy much more comfortable and your labor and delivery easier. This also provides good circulation in the legs, which prevents pooling of blood and helps to discourage varicose veins.

STARTING POSITION: Float on your back grasping the pool edge with both hands and resting your neck on the pool edge.

HOW TO DO IT: Perform 10 frog kicks. Then turn one quarter turn so that you are floating on your side as you grasp the pool edge, and perform

10 scissors kicks. Turn a quarter turn to a front float and do 10 prone frog kicks. Turn a quarter turn to your other side and do 10 scissors kicks. Breathe deeply and continuously, inhaling through your nose and exhaling through your mouth.

EXTRA TIPS: Vary the sequence and types of kicks you do. Make sure to include flutter kicks in your exercise.

EXERCISE: *Bicycle Pedal*
BENEFITS: Tones your lower body muscles. It is excellent for abdominal and "pushing" muscles.
STARTING POSITION: Float on your back, grasping the pool edge with both hands.
HOW TO DO IT: Alternately bend and straighten your legs as if you were pedaling a bicycle. Your knees should just break the surface of the water. Breathe deeply and continuously. Start with 25 repetitions or ½ minute of exercise.
EXTRA TIPS: If you want extra support, float in the corner of the pool, grasping each pool edge. You can make this exercise more demanding by using a flutter kick (in which the power comes from hip and thigh muscles) rather than a pedaling motion.

EXERCISE: *Leg Scissors*
BENEFITS: Stretches the muscles of the abdomen, upper legs, and inner thighs. This will really help when you are in the position to push.
STARTING POSITION: Stand with your back against the wall, grasping the pool edge with both hands. Raise both of your legs in front of you, keeping your toes pointed.
HOW TO DO IT: Spread your legs as far apart as possible, then cross your left leg over your right leg repeatedly. Follow this by crossing your right leg over your left leg repeatedly. Start with 5 repetitions per leg and increase the number as you become more comfortable.
EXTRA TIPS: Remember to breathe regularly by inhaling through your nose and exhaling through your mouth.

EXERCISE: *Leg and Inner Thigh Extension*
BENEFITS: Stretches and strengthens the inner thighs. This is very important because the pushing position places a great strain on this area. Conditioning of this area will help to prevent postpartum charley horses.
STARTING POSITION: Stand in waist-deep water, sideways to the pool wall. Grasp the pool edge with your inside hand.
HOW TO DO IT: Bring your outside knee up, keeping your toes pointed. When your knee is as high as is comfortable, turn your knee out; hold for

a moment, then slowly extend your leg with your knee turned out. Reverse the movements and bring your leg back to the starting position.

EXTRA TIPS: Breathe in through your nose and out through your mouth. Start with 6 repetitions for each leg.

EXERCISE: *Calf and Ankle Stretches*
BENEFITS: Stretches and strengthens the calf muscles, which will be of great help when you are in the pushing position.
STARTING POSITION: Stand in waist-deep water.
HOW TO DO IT:
- *Tiptoe stretch:* Face the pool wall and grasp the pool edge for balance. Lift yourself on tiptoes, stretching your calf muscles. Do both legs at once, and then do one leg at a time. Start with 10 repetitions.
- *Ankle stretches:* Alternately or simultaneously rotate your feet at the ankles. Rotate both clockwise and counterclockwise.

EXTRA TIPS: Try the tiptoe stretch on a step or ladder. Stand on the step or ladder on your toes, with your heels protruding over the edge. Stand on tiptoes and then lower your heels until they are below the ladder or step. Be sure to hold on to the pool wall, ladder, or railing for balance. What a great stretch!

EXERCISE: *Wide Knee Bends*
BENEFITS: Strengthens the thighs, buttocks, and calves and helps to tone pelvic muscles.
STARTING POSITION: Stand in waist-deep water, grasping the pool edge with both hands.
HOW TO DO IT: Bend your knees, spreading them as wide apart as is comfortable. Roll forward slightly so that your weight is balanced on the balls of your feet. Hold this position for 5 seconds, then rock back onto your heels. Straighten your legs until you are standing.
EXTRA TIPS: Consciously tighten your leg, stomach, and buttock muscles for a few seconds. Relax, and repeat. Start with 5 bends and increase as comfort allows. Inhale through your nose as your legs bend, and exhale through your mouth as they straighten.

EXERCISE: *Water Ballet Barre Exercises*
BENEFITS: These are terrific for stretching and toning your abdomen, lower back, legs, hips, and buttocks. They may make your pregnancy more comfortable, and they'll get your lower body in shape for labor and pushing.

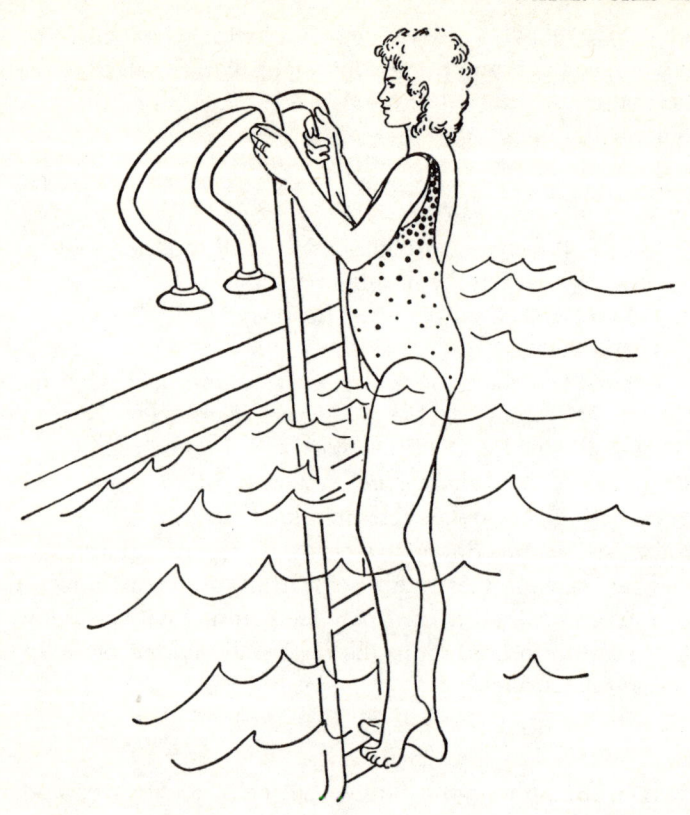

Tiptoe stretch on pool ladder.

    STARTING POSITION: Stand in the pool in waist-deep water.
    HOW TO DO IT:
• *Leg Lifts:* Face the pool wall and hold on to the pool edge with both hands. Raise your right leg straight out to the side as high as is comfortable, pointing your toes and using your thigh muscles to keep your knee straight. Then lower it. Start with 5 repetitions for each leg. Follow this by raising each leg straight to the rear, keeping your leg straight and your toes pointed. Begin with 5 repetitions for each leg. Next, turn and rest your back against the pool wall and grasp the pool edge with both hands. Raise each leg to the front, as high as is comfortable. Keep your toes pointed. Start with 5 repetitions. Breathe in through your nose each time you raise your leg and out through your mouth each time you lower your leg.

LOWER BODY WATERWORKS

Forward leg lift at pool's edge.

- *Lower Leg Stretch:* Face the pool wall, standing arm's length away. Grasp the edge, step forward with one foot, and shift your weight onto your forward leg, keeping your feet flat on the pool floor. In this lunge position, you will feel the gentle stretch in the calf of your back leg. Then reverse your legs. Try to keep your back leg straight; if the stretch is too much, bend your back knee slightly until you loosen. Close your eyes and breath deeply as you stretch.
- *Leg Swirl:* Stand sideways to the pool wall, grasping the pool edge with your inside hand. Lift your outside leg in front of you as high as is comfortable, keeping your toes pointed. Then slowly swing your leg around in a half circle until your leg is extended behind you. Then slowly swing your leg back to the front and lower it. Start with 5 repetitions, then turn around and try the other leg.

- *Foot Circles:* Stand sideways to the pool wall, grasping the pool edge with your inside hand. Lift your outside leg in front of you and trace a small circle in the water with your foot in a clockwise direction. Follow this with a circle traced in a counterclockwise direction. Start with 5 repetitions of each movement for each leg.
- *Double Leg Circles:* Stand with your back against the pool wall and grasp the pool edge with both hands. Place your feet together. Support yourself with your hands, lift your feet from the bottom, and circle in opposite directions with your legs. Then reverse the directions of the circles. Follow this by bringing your heels together and bending your knees outward in the Lamaze Tailor Sit (see p. 79). Start with 10 repetitions of each exercise.

EXTRA TIPS:
- Try the Ballet Barre Exercises with your feet flexed, as well as with your toes pointed; this will change the stretch.
- For extra stretch in the Leg Lifts, reach for your foot when you lift your leg to the front or side. Try reaching for your foot with either hand.
- If you find these exercises becoming too arduous, you may do a variation while you sit at the edge of the pool.

EXERCISE: *Wall Walk*

BENEFITS: Stretches all of the leg muscles. This exercise gets you into a position that is similar to your position with your legs in stirrups, which is sometimes used during labor and delivery. In addition, this exercise may help to relieve back strain.

STARTING POSITION: Stand in the pool facing the pool wall and grasp the pool edge with both hands.

HOW TO DO IT: Hold on to the pool edge and place your feet flat on the pool wall just above the pool floor. Slowly walk up on the wall, bending at the waist and knees. Try to touch your buttocks to the wall—this is similar to the stirrups position. Then return to standing by slowly walking your feet down the pool wall.

EXTRA TIPS: Do this exercise only with your doctor's approval and during the early stages of your pregnancy. As your pregnancy progresses, hold on to the pool edge, place both feet flat on the pool wall spread shoulder width apart just above the pool bottom, and bend and flex your legs.

EXERCISE: *Water Kegel*

BENEFITS: Isolates and strengthens the muscles of the pelvic and vaginal areas, which have extra stress during pregnancy.

LOWER BODY WATERWORKS

STARTING POSITION: Stand in chest-deep water.

HOW TO DO IT: Squeeze your lower abdominal muscles. Try to isolate and tighten the muscles of the urinary tract, vagina, and the rectum. Count slowly to five while holding.

EXTRA TIPS: This exercise is like the Kegel maneuver that is practiced in your prepared childbirth class. Also try this while treading water.

EXERCISE: *Lamaze Tailor Sit*

BENEFITS: Helps to strengthen the leg and groin muscles.

STARTING POSITION: Assume a sitting position in shallow water, with your back against the wall.

HOW TO DO IT: Sit with your legs crossed just below the surface of the water. Alternately cross your right leg over your left leg. As your legs bend at the knee, bring your feet up to the Tailor Sit.

EXTRA TIPS:

- A little note for the history buff: the tailor-sitting position (or Indian style) was used by cobblers of yesteryear while working.
- This Waterworks exercise can be easily done in the corner of the pool or in your home bathtub.

15

Total Body Waterworks

EXERCISE: *Bobbing with Aqua Jogging*

BENEFITS: Terrific aerobic exercises that provide extra oxygen for you and your child. They are also great for toning your entire body.

STARTING POSITION: Stand in neck-deep water, hands at your sides and your feet shoulder-width apart.

HOW TO DO IT:

- *Bobbing:* Bend your knees so that your head submerges, simultaneously raising your arms out to the sides. Keep your arms straight and your palms facing up. When your palms reach the surface of the water, turn them down. Push your arms back to your sides, and bounce off the pool bottom as you straighten your knees. Exhale continuously through your nose and mouth as you bend your knees, and while your face is submerged. Inhale through your nose as your legs straighten, once your face has emerged from the water. Start with 10 repetitions.
- *Aqua Jogging:* (You may wish to move to waist-deep water for this exercise.) Start at one side of the pool and jog to the other side, moving your arms at your sides as if you were running, but pushing the water as you go. Jog slowly and be careful of your balance. You may repeat laps, but don't overdo it.
- *Jogging in Place:* Jog in place. Scull with your hands at your sides to maintain your balance. Move forward, backward, and to the sides. Breathe deeply and continuously.

EXTRA TIPS:

- For that extra bounce, push off the pool bottom.

- *Bobbing:* Try bobbing with your knees spread wide and turned out (similar to the second position of ballet).
- *Aqua Jogging:* Try jogging backward through the water. (Look over your shoulder so that you don't run into anyone, and watch your balance.)

EXERCISE: *Arm and Leg Stretch*

BENEFITS: Stretches the back, calves, hamstrings, and arms. Helps you to focus and identify locations of tension and relaxation.

STARTING POSITION: Stand in waist-deep water facing the pool wall and far enough away so that you can grasp the pool edge when you bend at the waist.

HOW TO DO IT: Bend forward until your face reaches the water's surface, extend your arms, and grasp the pool edge. Tighten your thighs and straighten your knees. Then straighten your back and stretch your arms overhead. Lean to the left and then to the right as your arms are stretched overhead. Then lean forward at the waist, grasp the pool wall, and pull lightly to stretch again. Start with 10 repetitions.

EXTRA TIPS:
- For an extra stretch, lower your face and exhale in the water.
- Combine this exercise with deep cleansing breaths.

EXERCISE: *Leg Bend and Stretch*

BENEFITS: Tones and stretches the entire body, especially the trunk, arm, and upper leg muscles, which will be called into play during pushing.

STARTING POSITION: Stand in chest-deep water, sideways to the pool wall, holding on to the pool edge with your inside hand. Lean forward slightly.

HOW TO DO IT: Stretch your outside arm forward and upward as you bend your outside knee to bring your heel to your buttock; keep your outside foot pointed downward. Then reach back with your outside arm and grasp your ankle, stretching your muscles. Release your ankle and slowly return to the starting position. Repeat exercise on your other side. Start with 5 repetitions for each side.

EXTRA TIPS: Inhale slowly through your nose as you grasp your ankle and stretch, and exhale slowly through your mouth as you release and return.

EXERCISE: *Side Kick and Touch*

BENEFITS: Tones and stretches the entire body. Helps you to "loosen up." Limbering is essential to exercising and to prepared childbirth techniques.

STARTING POSITION: Stand in waist-deep water, sideways to the pool wall.

HOW TO DO IT: Grasp the pool edge with your inside hand and lift your outside hand overhead. Lift your inside leg, resting the ball of your foot on the pool edge. Bring your outside hand down and reach for your raised foot. Repeat the exercise on your other side. Start with 10 repetitions for each side.

EXTRA TIPS: If you're not flexible, begin with a bent knee position, in very shallow water. Or use a ladder or step for foot support.

EXERCISE: *Floating with Safe Recovery*

BENEFITS: Relaxes your entire body and stretches your lower back. It may help to relieve lower back pains, and it safely brings you back to a standing position from floating.

STARTING POSITION: Stand in chest-deep water and assume a prone (front down) or supine floating position.

HOW TO DO IT: From the prone float position, slowly bring your knees toward your chest and grasp your shins lightly with your hands, curling your back; then relax and streamline your entire body as you stretch in your floating position.

TO RECOVER: From the prone float position extend your arms forward and turn your hands so that your palms face downward. Simultaneously lift your head, pull your knees to your chest, and sweep your arms downward, pushing against the water. These actions will move your body into an upright position. Straighten your knees and stand. To recover from the back float position, extend your arms to the side at about a 45° angle to your head and turn your hands so that your palms face downward. Simultaneously drop your chin, pull your knees to your chest, and sweep your arms back, around, and upward through the water in a circular motion. When your body achieves an upright position, straighten your knees and stand.

EXTRA TIPS: Practice this safe recovery, since the ability to recover to a standing position is very important to your water safety.

EXERCISE: *Pendulum Body Swing*

BENEFITS: Tones and stretches the muscles of your entire body.

STARTING POSITION: Stand in neck-deep water facing the pool wall, your arms at your sides and your legs together.

HOW TO DO IT: Grasp the pool edge as you would for the bracket position, with your right hand above your left. Pull with your right arm, push with your left arm, and swing your legs sideways and upward toward your right arm. Then return to a vertical position. Next, push with your

TOTAL BODY WATERWORKS

left arm, pull with your right arm, and swing your legs sideways and upward toward your left arm. Start with 5 repetitions on each side. Inhale through your nose as you swing your legs and exhale through your mouth as you lower them.

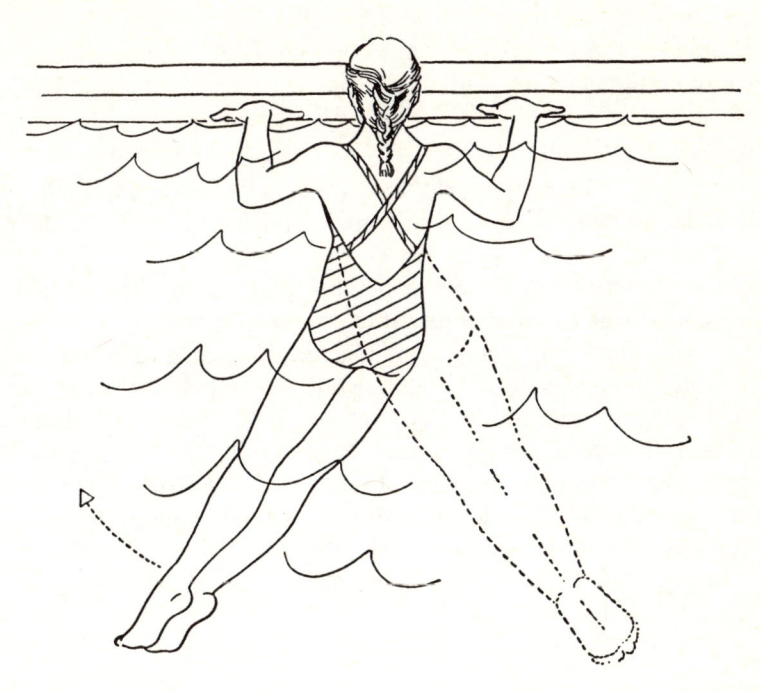

Pendulum body swing.

EXTRA TIPS: If swinging both legs is too taxing, try swinging one leg at a time.

EXERCISE: *Treading*

BENEFITS: This is a total body exercise as well as a great aerobic conditioner.

STARTING POSITION: Stand in neck-deep water.

HOW TO DO IT: Lean forward slightly in the water and bend your knees. Bounce off the pool bottom and begin a "bicycle" leg motion. Add a wide, slow sculling arm motion. Breathe continuously and deeply, inhaling through your nose and exhaling through your mouth.

EXTRA TIPS:
- Relaxed, slow treading movements are the most effective.
- Treading is not only a total body exercise, it is also a super deepwater safety skill. So enjoy and keep on treading!

- Try treading in the following ways: in a circle, clockwise and counterclockwise; forward; backward; sideways.
- Try different leg variations for treading: bicycle leg motion, frog kick, and scissors kick.
- Alternate bobbing and breathing with treading.
- Try treading alternately with your arms or legs alone.
- Tread with equipment: fins and/or paddles.

EXERCISE: *Pike's Pull*

BENEFITS: This exercise works the whole body. It is especially good for toning the abdominal, back, and upper thigh muscles. It also helps to develop concentration and body control.

STARTING POSITION: Assume the bracket position in chest-deep water with your body turned so that you float in a prone position.

HOW TO DO IT: Using your abdominal muscles, pike, i.e., bend at the waist, keeping your legs straight, until your feet touch the wall. (If you can't bend this far comfortably, bend only as far as you can.) Bend your knees in and arch your back to return your legs to the starting position. Keep your feet flexed throughout the exercise. Exhale through your mouth as you pike, and inhale through your nose as you straighten. Start with 5 repetitions and increase to as many as you can do comfortably.

EXTRA TIPS: Concentrate on moving slowly and stretching every part of your body. You'll feel terrific!

EXERCISE: *Posture Check*

BENEFITS: Helps in body alignment and relieves strain on back muscles.

STARTING POSITION: Stand in waist-deep water with your back and hips against the pool wall.

HOW TO DO IT: Grasp the pool edge with both hands. Bend your knees and place your feet flat against the pool wall, supporting yourself. Keep your arms straight. Hold for a count of 10; rest; repeat.

EXTRA TIPS: You can also practice a variation of this exercise at home. Lie on the floor with your knees bent, feet flat on the floor. Arch your back slowly and lift your hips off the floor. Inhale through your nose as you lift your hips and exhale through your mouth as you lower your hips.

EXERCISE: *Total Body Focal Relaxation*

BENEFITS: Teaches you how to relax and control your body. This will make you more comfortable throughout your pregnancy as well as during

TOTAL BODY WATERWORKS 85

labor and delivery. Tension can be a big problem during labor. This technique is helpful in learning to relax more.

STARTING POSITION: Stand in neck-deep water with your back against the pool wall.

HOW TO DO IT:
- Try to relax all of the muscles of your body by focusing on each body part and consciously relaxing. Start by closing your eyes and thinking about relaxing all of the muscles of your head and neck. Then move through the other parts of your body from the neck down. Breathe deeply and slowly, inhaling through your nose and exhaling through your mouth.
- Try to use this relaxation technique while floating on your back. Then stretch out as far as possible while floating.

EXTRA TIPS:
- After you have relaxed your body, focus on contracting and then relaxing one muscle at a time. Then combine different muscles in contraction and relaxation.
- Practice different breathing patterns with this relaxation exercise.
- This exercise may be practiced at home.
- Remember: the better you can control your body and relax, the easier your labor and delivery will be.

EXERCISE: *Effleurage*

BENEFITS: This exercise is essential to many prepared childbirth techniques. It has a wonderfully soothing, relaxing effect. This gives an external sensation of pleasure that can be more easily perceived than the internal contraction.

STARTING POSITION: Stand in the pool or float on your back.

HOW TO DO IT: Place your fingers on your navel, pointed slightly downward. Trace a circular design on your abdomen with your fingertips in a continuous motion.

EXTRA TIPS: Use effleurage between Waterworks exercises and with different breathing patterns.

16

At-Home Waterworks

Even if you can't get to your swimming pool, you can enjoy some of the benefits of exercising in a water environment by using your sink, tub, or shower. (Note: it is *not* advisable to use whirlpools, saunas, steamrooms, or Turkish baths during your pregnancy.) The following are some examples of home sink or basin, tub, or shower water exercises that you can do at any time.

Be certain that the bottom of the tub has a non-slip surface.

Sink or Washbasin Exercise

Sit in a comfortable position in your bathroom or kitchen with your chest level with the sink or washbasin. Fill the sink with lukewarm water to about two-thirds full or with enough water to cover your face. (Be careful not to fill it too full, or the water will spill over the sides.) Try these exercises.

EXERCISE: *Bobbing and/or Rhythmic Breathing*
BENEFITS: This exercise will allow you to practice breathing patterns used in swimming and prepared childbirth.
STARTING POSITION: Sit comfortably over the sink with your chin at the surface of the water.
HOW TO DO IT: With your face out of the water, inhale deeply

through your nose; then lower your face into the water to hairline level and exhale fully through your nose and mouth. Repeat.

EXTRA TIPS:
- Practice your rhythmic breathing by turning your face to one side for inhalation. Vary by alternating sides.
- Practice your various breathing patterns for prepared childbirth (see breathing chart).

Bathtub and Shower Exercises

EXERCISE: *Effleurage with Cleansing Breath*
BENEFITS: Relaxes tense muscles and provides relaxation for active muscles. This also provides external stimuli in a pleasant fashion.
STARTING POSITION: Lie back against the back of the tub so that your hands are free. Begin and end with a cleansing breath.
HOW TO DO IT: Relax all parts of your body and do your effleurage. This is a circular, fingertip massage, beginning with placing both your hands at your hairline. Simultaneously inhale and make semicircles ending at your breastbone. Exhale and complete the circle inward, finishing at your hairline.
EXTRA TIPS: Try to isolate each body part and consciously relax it.

EXERCISE: *Tailor Sit*
BENEFITS: Stretches the inner thighs and pelvic floor muscles.
STARTING POSITION: Sit in the tub with your back against the side of the tub. Bend your knees, drawing your feet close to your crotch with the soles of your feet together or your ankles crossed one over the other, Indian style.
HOW TO DO IT: Gently lean forward and press your elbows to the inside of your knees to stretch.
EXTRA TIPS:
- Massage your feet by placing your thumbs on your arches and your fingers on top of your feet and rocking gently from side to side.
- With cleansing breath, inhale as you sit, exhale as you bend.
- *Tailor Press Variation:* Place the soles of your feet together, grasping your ankles. Place your elbows on your knees. Gently roll forward, keeping your back straight, and gently press your knees toward the bottom of the tub with your elbows.

EXERCISE: *Sitting Leg Bends*
BENEFITS: Strengthens the legs and the abdomen.

STARTING POSITION: While sitting in the tub, place your hands on the tub bottom beside your hips, extend your left leg, and bend your right knee, keeping your right foot flat on the tub's bottom.

HOW TO DO IT: Bend your left leg and straighten your right leg at the same time. Alternate legs.

EXTRA TIPS: Bring both knees up to a tuck position, then roll from one side to the other.

EXERCISE: *Feet Flex*
BENEFITS: Stretches the calf muscles.
STARTING POSITION: With your knees straight, sit back in the tub.

HOW TO DO IT: Flex your feet and point your toes toward the ceiling, then point your toes forward.

EXTRA TIPS: Keep your knees straight, and as you flex, your heels should lift off the bottom of the tub. Inhale as you flex, exhale as you straighten.

EXERCISE: *Shoulder Shrugs*
BENEFITS: Helps to relieve tension and relax your shoulders and neck.
STARTING POSITION: You can do this sitting in the tub while taking a bath or standing in the tub while taking a shower.

HOW TO DO IT: Raise and lower both shoulders simultaneously, and then alternately, raising and lowering one shoulder at a time.

EXTRA TIPS:
- Rotate your shoulders forward and backward alternately, and then simultaneously.
- Raise your shoulders and roll your head forward, then lower your shoulders and roll your head backward.

EXERCISE: *Pelvic Tilt*
BENEFITS: Strengthens the back and the abdominal muscles. This is especially helpful during pregnancy, if you experience low back discomfort, and it strengthens muscles used during pushing.

STARTING POSITION: Lie flat on your back in the tub, resting on your elbows with your knees bent and your feet and buttocks flat on the tub's bottom.

HOW TO DO IT: Press the small of your back toward the bottom of the tub, tilting your pelvis upward. Round your shoulders and leave your head down. Hold this position momentarily and then slowly relax back to the starting position to a slow count of 5. Rest and repeat.

EXTRA TIPS: This is a good toner for your back muscles during your postpartum period.

AT-HOME WATERWORKS

EXERCISE: *Kegel*

BENEFITS: Strengthens the perineal and pelvic floor muscles, and develops collateral circulation, which aids in the healing of the episiotomy and/or helps relieve discomfort of hemorrhoids during postpartum recovery; it also helps to identify different parts of the body with tensing and relaxation, which helps in pushing.

STARTING POSITION: Stand while showering or sit in the tub while bathing.

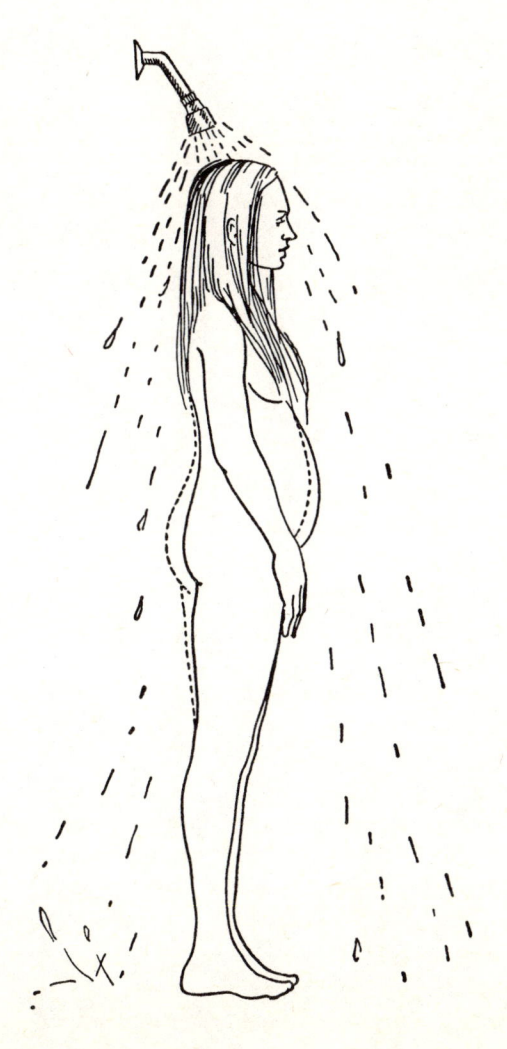

Practice Kegel exercise during shower.

HOW TO DO IT: Contract the muscles in your pelvic floor area and buttocks between your rectum and vagina for a count of 5. Then release your muscles, and repeat 5 times.

EXTRA TIPS: Check yourself when urinating by trying to stop the flow of urine midstream. Then go to a vaginal contraction and on to a rectal contraction in a continuous progression.

III

Pregnancy Swim Program

17

Introduction

    This section of the book outlines a swimming exercise program for you to practice during your pregnancy. Here are some general tips.

1. Start your exercise program gradually, especially if you are not accustomed to exercising. You will be more comfortable and derive more benefit if you start out slowly and then expand your program as your muscle tone and aerobic capacity improve.
2. Generally, pregnant women find that certain swimming strokes are more comfortable than others. Experiment to see which strokes fit your body during the different stages of your pregnancy. You may find that the crawl stroke and the breaststroke, as well as easy flutter kicking while holding on to the wall or a kickboard, are most suitable as your pregnancy advances. The butterfly stroke may be too strenuous; and the backstroke, while suitable during the early stages of your pregnancy, may not be a good stroke during your later stages, because it may not be comfortable.
3. Each water exercise session has three parts: a warm-up, a main swim, and a stretch-out. Your warm-up, which takes approximately five minutes, prepares your body for exercising. A good warm-up makes the exercises themselves more comfortable. The main swim is the central part of the exercise session, in which you improve your muscle tone, breathing capacity, and flexibility. It should last from ten to twenty minutes. For each main swim, there are three sets of exercises of varying intensity, one each for those accustomed to occasional, regular, or fre-

quent exercise. Select the set that is appropriate to your fitness level and comfort. Don't hesitate to switch levels whenever you wish to change the rigor of your program.

Level	Appropriate for	Frequency of Workout	Timed Swim	Main Swim	Total Swim Time
1	Occasional Exerciser	1 time/wk	25 yards in 1 minute	10 min.	20 min.
2	Regular Exerciser	2 times/wk	50 yards in 1½ minutes	15 min.	25 min.
3	Fitness/Frequent Exerciser	3 times/wk or daily	50 yards in 1 minute	20 min.	30 min. (or more)

The stretch-out or cool-down will help keep your body loose and limber, and it will bring your body back to a relaxed state after exercising. It should take about five minutes.

The Program—Purpose of the Program

- To help you get in shape and stay in shape, to help you relax, and to instill a feeling of well-being.
- To help build your aerobic capacity. (This is important not only for your general health and for your comfort in childbirth, but it also complements prepared childbirth methods, which use breathing exercises closely related to the breathing exercises in this program.)
- To prepare your muscles (including those directly involved in childbirth) for labor and delivery.

Length of the Program

This swim program is designed to span the length of your pregnancy. It is divided into three parts to correspond with the trimesters of your pregnancy.

The human gestation period (the term of your pregnancy) is approximately 40 weeks. However, when your doctor tells you your estimated date of confinement (EDC) or due date, there is usually a 2 week uncertainty either way (i.e., 38 to 42 weeks). As you can calculate, your pregnancy will not last exactly 9 calendar months (it's more like 10 lunar months). Although there is no reason to avoid swimming in your ninth month, check with your doctor. Should your membranes (bag of waters) begin to rupture, stop swimming.

INTRODUCTION

This program begins in the fifth week of your pregnancy, since by that time you will have confirmed your pregnancy and checked with your doctor about this program.

How to Begin

The first part of this program is progressive; your swim sessions gradually increase in content during your first two trimesters. In your third trimester, your workouts will decrease in time as well as intensity.

Waterworks exercises are also integrated into this program, and you should include these as an integral part of your warm-up and stretch-out.

The postpartum program helps you get back into shape after birth and includes synchronized swimming.

When to Swim

You may exercise one day per week or daily—it depends on you and how you feel. Try to swim every other day, or at least two to three times per week, to achieve maximum benefit.

You can swim morning, noon, or night—whenever you prefer. Swim whenever you feel best; if you experience bouts of morning sickness, it is preferable to swim when you are feeling better. Don't forget that this program may help you through the uncomfortable parts of your pregnancy.

During your first trimester, you may feel quite fatigued because of the hormonal and other physiological changes your body is undergoing. If you require more sleep, you'll feel better and keep your spirits up if you swim. Adjust your swim sessions to your own schedule and try to swim when you're not rushed. Even if you feel tired or uncomfortable before you swim, the water and exercise will make you feel better.

During your second trimester, your body will have adjusted to the changes of the first trimester and swimming will become easier. During your third trimester, although you will be larger, you will still be able to swim and exercise.

How Often You Should Swim

Remember, you should design your swimming schedule to suit your needs—swim from one to five times per week.

Reminder

For your swimming and exercise program to be effective, it should include the following components:

- *Frequency* Try to swim at least two times per week; three times per week is ideal for most people, but even once a week is okay.
- *Intensity* Your exercise session should move from easy (warm-up) to vigorous exercise (main swim), and back to easy (stretch-out). (Note: intensity is *relative*, that is, it should vary with the stage of your pregnancy and your level of fitness.)
- *Progression* Start out with easy skills and build up to more demanding ones.

Extra Bonus Reminder

- *Encouragement* If possible, swim with a buddy, because encouragement and support from family and friends is 90 percent of the battle. Of course, if you can't find a partner, you still can have a great time swimming alone.

Equipment

To start with you will need:

A *swimsuit* In your first trimester, your regular swimsuit will be adequate, since your weight gain is usually minimal. In your second trimester, you may need a larger size or one that will stretch. In your third trimester, use a leotard, a larger stretch suit, or a maternity-styled suit.

A *cap* If the pool regulations require one or if you choose to wear one, I suggest the following. If your hair is long, a cap made of Lycra rather than latex is easier to tuck your hair up into. If you wish to keep your hair dry, wear a latex cap over the Lycra cap.

A *pair of goggles* Goggles are not absolutely necessary, but they do keep chlorine from bothering your eyes and improve vision in the water. They'll open a whole new underwater world to you. There are many different styles, and I suggest you try them on to find one that is comfortable. Most goggles adjust at the nose piece and/or the head strap for comfort and a watertight fit. If you wish, you can even buy goggles with prescription lenses, although you'll find that ordinary goggles in the water have a magnifying effect that ameliorates nearsightedness.

Optional Equipment There are several pieces of equipment you can use to add variety to your swimming. Many facilities have this equipment available for use by swimmers.
- A kickboard is a flat flotation device that you can use to support your body while kicking or doing other exercises that I will describe later.
- A pull buoy is a small flotation device that you can use to support your legs while practicing your arm strokes.
- Swim fins are large paddles that attach to your feet. They are great for exercising your hips and legs because they greatly increase the resistance of the water to your kicks (which, by the way, will make you fly through the water). Swim fins work best with the flutter kick.
- Hand paddles are paddles that attach to your hands to increase the resistance of the water to your arm strokes. They work similarly to swim fins and are great for strengthening your arms and shoulders.

Pace Clocks Most swimming facilities are equipped with a large timing clock with a sweep second hand, called a pace clock. This clock is ideal for timing your swims and rest periods. Learning to use the clock will also prepare you to time your labor contractions.

If your facility does not have a pace clock it may have a large wall clock with a sweep second hand that you can use for timing.

If possible, obtain a waterproof digital watch with functions for seconds and a stopwatch, which you can wear while swimming. This will be a great help in timing.

The Pool Most pools are measured in yards or in meters. You can adjust your swim session to accommodate either. The following measurements will be helpful.
- 400 meters = ¼ mile (440 yards)
- 800 meters = ½ mile (880 yards)
- In a 20-yard pool:
    22 laps = ¼ mile
    44 laps = ½ mile
- In a 25-yard pool:
    18 laps = ¼ mile
    36 laps = ½ mile
- In a 50-meter pool:
    8 laps = ¼ mile
    16 laps = ½ mile

Pools range from the classic rectangular, fifty-meter Olympic style to the weird kidney shape. You can use any size or shape pool for your swim sessions although you may have to adjust your exercises slightly to fit the pool.

Take advantage of pool amenities such as water jets that give a relaxing massage while you float in the water.

Safety Points

- Check with your doctor on a periodic basis to keep him or her fully advised of your exercise program.
- If you should experience any discomfort or pain, slow down and take it easy. If the discomfort and pain are more than the "kinks" expected from exercising muscles conditioned to a sedentary life, or if discomfort continues, stop exercising and check with your doctor.
- Be careful while walking in the pool area—the deck may be slippery when wet.
- Listen to your body—stop swimming if you feel too cold, too hot, or too tired.

Swim Tips and Courtesy

- If you swim in a pool divided into lanes, choose a lane that is appropriate to your swimming speed.
- When lap swimming, stay to the right of the lane and pass slower swimmers at the wall.
- When resting at poolside, stay clear of swimmers who are making turns.

Where to Swim—How to Find Your Watering Hole

Look for a swimming facility that:

- is quiet, clean, and safe.
- has ample locker space.
- has sitting space and a lounge area.
- has family swim sessions—make swimming a family affair.
- has other services, for example, massages for relaxation.
- has a water temperature of about 80° F.

About Stretching

Your body needs strength, but it also needs flexibility. Muscles tend to shorten and tighten if you do not use them properly, so it is important to warm-up before your swim and to stretch-out at the finish of your swim. Include stretching in your warm-up and stretch-out. Each stretching session should last at least five minutes.

There are several basic types of stretching movements:

- *Ballistic movement*, in which you forcefully bounce up and down to stretch the muscles.
- *Passive movement*, in which someone helps you to increase your range of motion; that is, to complete the stretch.
- *Contraction and relaxation movement*, in which you push against an opposing muscle mass. (For example, a hamstring stretch will help to offset an overly strong thigh muscle.)
- *Slow progressive stretch*, in which you go to your maximum comfortable extension and gently try to extend your stretch for about thirty seconds. This is the best type of stretch, and it can be done in the water.

Breathe regularly and deeply so that oxygen can reach your muscles while you stretch. You can space your stretching sessions throughout the day (you can even stretch while watching television). I've described specific stretching exercises for you in the next chapter of this book in the warm-up skills section.

Reminders

- Rest when necessary.
- For variety, change strokes or use equipment such as a kickboard or hand paddles.
- Your resting time between laps should depend on your comfort, fatigue, and ability level.
- Take adequate rest periods between exercises and swims in your program. Do not push yourself too hard. Your exercise should be mildly challenging but not too taxing. As your pregnancy progresses, give yourself extra rest.
- First and foremost—*safety first!* Never overexert yourself and always use caution! Listen at all times to your body! Keep your doctor informed.

ENJOY YOURSELF!

18

Trimester 1

Your first trimester is a very exciting time. You will be emotionally adjusting to the fact that your family will be growing. During this adjustment, don't forget to get yourself ready mentally and physically by conditioning your body. Find time to relieve any tension with a relaxing swim.

Your first trimester swimming program commences with the fifth week of pregnancy, on the assumption that at the fifth week, you will have obtained your doctor's confirmation that you are pregnant and his or her approval to begin this program. However, you may begin this program at any time before or during your pregnancy.

There are minor discomforts you may experience during your first trimester of pregnancy such as fatigue, occasional nausea, and frequent urination. Swimming as often as you can may help you feel better and more fit during this first trimester.

The first trimester program includes the following highlights:

- General conditioning for fitness with different strokes.
- Use of goggles.
- Swimming and Waterworks for conditioning, strength, and flexibility.
- Timed swims.
- Treading and sculling.
- Stroke counts.
- Rhythmic and alternate breathing (these are explained in chapter 11).

First Trimester General Tips

Warm-Up Skills: These warm-up skills may be used as part of or all of your warm-ups and stretch-outs in the first trimester.

- *On-Deck Sitting:*

Sit on the pool deck, relax, and let the water refresh your feet and legs by extending your legs into the water and flexing and extending your toes. Do the following:

    10 foot circles right and left,

    10 breaststroke kicks,

    flutter kicks (10 easy, 10 moderate, 10 vigorous, 10 moderate, and 10 easy).

- *Entering the Water:*

Enter the water gently and gracefully. Use the ladder or steps or try this entry: sit on the deck with your legs in the water, place your hands outside your hips at the pool edge, press away, and make a quarter turn as you slip into the water. Do not jump or dive into the pool while you're pregnant.

- *Breathing:*

This breathing exercise will complement breathing exercises taught in prepared childbirth classes. (It is similar to the cleansing breath used in the Lamaze prepared childbirth method.)

    Stand in the pool and hold on to the wall for balance. Inhale through your nose slowly and deeply. Exhale through your mouth slowly and fully. Keep in mind that during your regular swim, you should use both your nose and mouth for inhaling and exhaling.

- *Bobbing:*

Stand in chest-deep water with your feet shoulder-width apart. Keep your knees turned outward (ballet lovers know this is similar to the second position) to open up your pelvic cavity and to stretch the muscles of your inner leg. (This is similar to the tailor position used in childbirth exercises.) Bend your knees to lower your body in the water until your chin touches the surface; then straighten your knees. Repeat. As your pregnancy progresses, you'll need a little assistance for both submerging and balancing.

    TIPS:

    Hold on to the side of the pool with one hand and extend the other hand to the side at your hip level. Use your palm to press the water upward to help you submerge. You can also bob with a partner and help each other submerge.

- *Combined Bobbing and Breathing:*

Here you are coordinating breathing with physical action, a skill that you will use during labor and delivery. With practice, you won't have to think about combining breathing with movement, and you'll help to improve your aerobic fitness.

- *Controlled Breathing While Bobbing (Knee Bends):*

Start your aerobic conditioning here! Practice inhaling and exhaling through both your mouth and your nose. Inhale through your mouth as though you are drinking through a straw and simultaneously inhale through your nose as if you are smelling a terrific dish. Exhale through your mouth as if cooling a cup of hot coffee and simultaneously exhale through your nose as if you are sneezing. Add warm-up bobbing to your breathing. Inhale on the way down, exhale as you straighten. Do 10 repetitions, rest, and repeat.

- *Relaxed Wall Flutter Kicks:*

Hold on to the edge of the pool while you flutter kick gently against the water's resistance. Exaggerate your leg action with knee bends. This exercise will help to tone your legs.

- *Towel Stretch:*

After showering, or after your swim, while you're still wet, twist a towel loosely and hold it behind your back with both hands. Reach overhead and stretch side to side. Then, move the towel slowly back and forth behind your back. Finish your towel stretch by applying your favorite moisturizing lotion. This procedure helps to keep your skin in tip-top condition.

First Trimester Level—Week 5

SWIM POINTERS:

- Swim for conditioning (resting as needed).
- Introduction to timing your swims.

REMINDERS:

Select the swim session that is right for you. Be sure you have received your doctor's approval before starting this program. Always keep in mind, for your comfort and safety, the following rule: *LISTEN TO YOUR BODY!*

WARM-UP:

1 minute of bobbing.
1 minute of rhythmic breathing.
1 minute of combined bobbing and breathing.
1 minute of kicking.
1 minute of arm pulls in place.

MAIN SWIM:

Level 1

A 10-minute swim, pausing every lap (e.g., 25 yards), or as needed. Use the crawl or another stroke.

Level 2

A 15-minute swim, pausing every 2 laps (e.g., 50 yards) or as needed. Use the crawl or other stroke.

Level 3

A 20-minute swim, pausing every 4 laps (e.g., 100 yards) or as needed. Use the crawl or other stroke.

STRETCH-OUT:

2 minutes of the walking crawl stroke.
3 minutes of stretching on the wall and relaxed floating.

First Trimester Level—Week 6

SWIM POINTERS:

• How to use goggles.
• Using bobbing while resting between laps.

REMINDER:

Goggles give you better vision in the water, and they give your eyes protection against the chlorine. Goggles take a bit of time to get used to, so be patient.

WARM-UP:

Adjust your goggles for comfort.
1 minute of bobbing and breathing with your goggles on.
2 minutes of kicking in bracket position against the wall—from easy to moderate and back to easy.
1 minute of crawl stroke in place or walking.
1 minute of crawl stroke with rhythmic breathing.

MAIN SWIM:

Level 1

A 10-minute swim using the crawl stroke, bobbing 10 times in place after each 25 yards, or 1 lap.

Level 2

A 15-minute swim using the crawl stroke, bobbing 10 times in place after each 50 yards or 2 laps.

Level 3

A 20-minute swim using the crawl stroke, bobbing 10 times in place after every 100 yards or 4 laps.

STRETCH-OUT:

Walking crawl stroke; breaststroke; floating; and Waterworks.

First Trimester Level—Week 7

SWIM POINTER:

• Using a timing device* for 50-yard swims.

REMINDER:

You may wish to record your swim times at the end of your swim session on the chart provided.

WARM-UP:

1 minute of bobbing and breathing.
2 minutes of sidestroke and/or scissors kick holding on to the wall in bracket position.
2 minutes of crawl stroke.

MAIN SWIM:

Level 1
  A 3-minute continuous swim, resting as needed.
  Rest for 2 minutes.
  A timed swim of 1 × 50 yards.
  Rest one minute.
  A timed swim of 1 × 50 yards.

Level 2
  A 5-minute continuous swim, resting as needed.
  Rest for 3 minutes.
  3 × 50 yard timed swims.
  Rest one minute between the 50-yard swims.

Level 3
  An 8-minute continuous swim, resting as needed.
  Rest for 3 minutes.
  4 × 50 yard timed swims.
  Rest one minute between the 50-yard swims.

* A timing device is either a pace clock or a regular clock. You start each new swim at the 60-second mark or when the second hand is at the top of the clock. Swim 2 laps or 50 yards.

STRETCH-OUT:

    1 minute of bobbing.
    3 Waterworks stretches of your choice.
    1 minute of kicking.

First Trimester Level—Week 8

SWIM POINTER:

· Interval swimming. Interval swimming is a series of swims of equal distance done within a specified period of time so that you commence each swim in a certain time interval. For example, 50 yards done "on" (within) 2 minutes and then repeated one or more times.

REMINDER:

Try to alternate your strokes. For example, alternate the crawl stroke and the sidestroke.

WARM-UP:

1 minute of bobbing and kicking.
2 minutes of sidestroke kicking on the wall.
1 minute of sidestroke.
1 minute of crawl stroke.

MAIN SWIM:

Level 1
A 5-minute swim.
Rest for 2 minutes.
Swim 2 × 50 yards on 2 minutes.

Level 2
A 7-minute swim.
Rest for 2 minutes.
Swim 3 × 50 yards on 2 minutes.

Level 3
A 10-minute swim.
Rest for 2 minutes.
Swim 4 × 50 yards on 2 minutes.

STRETCH-OUT:

3 Waterworks of your choice.
2 minutes of easy kicking.

First Trimester Level—Week 9

SWIM POINTER:

· Stroke-count, that is, keeping the number of strokes consistent per lap.

REMINDER:

You should keep count of your strokes as your fingertips enter the water (for the catch of each stroke); stretch out and get the most glide from each arm motion.

WARM-UP:

Choose any 5 Waterworks exercises.

MAIN SWIM:

Level 1
A 5-minute continuous swim—vary your strokes.
Rest for 2 minutes.
Swim 4 × 25 yards on 1 minute. Count the number of strokes per lap and try to keep that number constant for each lap.

Level 2
A 10-minute continuous swim—vary your strokes.
Rest for 2 minutes.
Swim 4 × 25 yards on 1 minute. Count the number of strokes per lap and try to keep that number constant for each lap.

Level 3
A 15-minute continuous swim—vary your strokes.
Rest for 2 minutes.
Swim 4 × 25 yards on 1 minute. Count the number of strokes per lap and try to keep that number constant for each lap.

STRETCH-OUT:

Choose any 5 Waterworks exercises.

First Trimester Level—Week 10

SWIM POINTERS:

- Treading—using wide sculling arm motion with a frog kick.
- 100-yard interval swim.

REMINDER:

Try to keep your time consistent for each of your 100-yard swims.

WARM-UP:

1 minute of bobbing and breathing.
2 minutes of sculling arm motion in chest-deep water.
1 minute of frog kicks at the wall.
1 minute of treading water in place—combine arm and leg motion.

MAIN SWIM:

Level 1
A 3-minute continuous swim—vary your strokes.
Rest as needed.
Tread water for 1 minute.
Rest as needed.
Swim 2 × 100 yards on 4 minutes.

Level 2
A 5-minute continuous swim—vary your strokes.
Rest as needed.
Tread water for 1 to 2 minutes.
Rest as needed.
Swim 2 × 100 yards on 3 minutes.

Level 3
A 10-minute continuous swim—vary your strokes.
Rest as needed.
Tread water for 1 to 3 minutes.

Rest as needed.
Swim 3 × 100 yards on 3 minutes.

STRETCH-OUT:

Alternate treading water with the back or prone float.
Choose 3 Waterworks.

First Trimester Level—Week 11

SWIM POINTER:

· Alternate breathing. Alternate breathing is a variation of rhythmic breathing. You alternate your head movements from right to left with every 3 arm motions, breathing on every 3 strokes instead of every 2. This will help develop your aerobic capacity.

REMINDER:

Try your alternate breathing on odd-numbered laps during your continuous swim.

WARM-UP:

Practice alternate breathing while standing and then while you are walking.
Choose any 3 Waterworks exercises.

MAIN SWIM:

Level 1
  Swim 4 × 25 yards on 1 minute.
  Rest as needed.

Level 2
  A 10-minute continuous swim. (Try alternate breathing on every odd-numbered lap.)
  Tread water for 1 to 2 minutes.
  Rest as needed.
  Swim 4 × 25 yards on 1 minute.

Level 3
  A 10-minute continuous swim with alternate breathing on every odd-numbered lap.
  Tread water for 1 to 3 minutes.

Rest as needed.
Swim 4 × 50 yards on 2 minutes.

STRETCH-OUT:

Choose any 3 Waterworks exercises and review alternate breathing.

First Trimester Level—Week 12

SWIM POINTER:

• Using sculling arm motion during part of your swim session.

REMINDERS:

When sculling, your hands should be close to your hips. Your hands should move outward from your body using equal motion.
Flexing your wrists will enable you to move forward.

WARM-UP:

Practice sculling, first standing and then walking backward across the width of the pool.

MAIN SWIM:

Level 1
A 5-minute continuous swim using alternate breathing as much as possible.
Rest as needed.
Scull 2 laps with flutter kicking—rest between the laps.
Rest as needed.
Swim 2 × 25 yards on 1 minute with a crawl stroke count.

Level 2
A 10-minute continuous swim using alternate breathing as much as possible.
Rest as needed.
Scull 2 laps with flutter kicking—rest between the laps.
Swim 2 × 25 yards on 1 minute with a crawl stroke count.

Level 3
A 15-minute swim varying your strokes and using alternate breathing as much as possible.
Rest as needed.

Scull 2 laps with flutter kicking.
Swim 2 × 25 yards on 1 minute with a crawl stroke count.

STRETCH-OUT:

Choose 3 Waterworks.
Practice sculling and review treading leg motions for treading skill.

CHARTING YOUR SWIMS: PERSONAL SWIM LOG

TRIMESTER 1

Week/Date	Pool Location and Length	Warm-Up	Main Swim	Stretch-Out	Total Time/ Distance of Workout	Weight	Comments
5							
6							
7							
8 28/3 29/3	Fulham Pools 25 metres " "	3 mins 5 mins	10 lengths 20 mins (wk 8)	5 mins 5 mins	20 mins 30 mins	10/9 13.5	First swim Pd 4+5 wks etc.
9 3/4 6/4	" " " "	5 mins of deterents " "	20 mins (wk 8) etc. " "	5 mins of deterents " " wets etc.	30 mins 30 mins " "	10/9 10.5 10/10	Repeat etc. etc.
10 8/4 12/4	" " " "	Twelve " "	5k to " "	" " " "	" " " "	10/10 " "	" "
11 15/4 19/4	" " " "	Five " "	Decreased !!! Better " " OK	etc etc etc " "	30 mins " " " "	10/11 " "	Alt. breathing difficult 5+ better Feeling fitter
12 22/4 24/4 28/4	" " " " " "	" " " " " "	" " " " " "	" " " " " "	" " " " " "	10/10 " " 10/12!!	Bicental loss! wks

19
Trimester 2

By the time you reach your second trimester, you'll have a good start toward fitness—if you've followed the first trimester program. You will be more fit, stronger, more flexible, and more comfortable with basic swimming skills. The second trimester swimming program builds on the first, introducing more advanced swimming skills and exercises.

The following are the highlights of the second trimester swimming program:

- Review of swimming strokes—breaststroke, sidestroke, and backstroke variations.
- Introduction to medley of strokes.
- Timed swims on different time intervals.
- Lap counts for distance swims.
- Pyramid swims.
- Fartlek (alternating easy and moderate pace) swims.
- Introduction to cleansing breath.

Second Trimester—Week 13

SWIM POINTER:

· Lap count for your continuous 5-, 10-, and 15-minute swims.

REMINDER:

Record the number of laps you do during your continuous swim and note the strokes used.

WARM-UP:

Choose 4 Waterworks.
Practice alternate breathing standing in shallow water.

MAIN SWIM:

Level 1
A 5-minute continuous swim—count and record your laps.
Rest as needed.
Tread water for 1 minute.
Rest as needed.
1 × 50 yards sidestroke.

Level 2
A 10-minute continuous swim—count and record your laps.
Rest as needed.
Tread water for 1 or 2 minutes.
Rest as needed.
1 × 50 yards sidestroke.

Level 3
A 15-minute continuous swim—count and record your laps and strokes.
Tread water for 1 to 2 minutes.
Rest as needed.
1 × 50 yards sidestroke.

STRETCH-OUT:

Choose 5 Waterworks.

Second Trimester—Week 14

SWIM POINTER:

• Pyramid swim—a sequence of increasing then decreasing distances with one-minute rest periods between each.

REMINDER:

Begin each new swim one minute after you've finished, e.g., if you've completed your first 2 laps in 55 seconds, begin the next swim in one minute when the second hand reaches 55 again.

WARM-UP:

Rhythmic breathing.
Medley of pyramid kicks at the wall:
• Side kick—25 times
• Prone flutter kick—50 times
• Back kick—25 times.

MAIN SWIM:

Level 1

Swim the following yards: 25-50-100-50-25, i.e.,
1 × 25 yards
1 × 50 yards
1 × 100 yards
1 × 50 yards
1 × 25 yards.
Rest 1 minute between swims.

Level 2

Swim the following yards: 50-100-150-100-50, i.e.,
1 × 50 yards
1 × 100 yards
1 × 150 yards
1 × 100 yards
1 × 50 yards.
Rest one minute between swims.

TRIMESTER 2

Level 3

Swim the following yards: 50-100-150-200-150-100-50, i.e.,

    1 × 50 yards   6 laps (3 double)   Post 9 yds
    1 × 100 yards   12 laps (6 double)
    1 × 150 yards   18 laps / 9 double
    1 × 200 yards   24 laps (12 double)
    1 × 150 yards   18 laps (9 double)
    1 × 100 yards   12 laps (6 double)
    1 × 50 yards.   6 laps (3 double)

Rest one minute between swims.

(handwritten dates in margin: 12/5/91, 15/5/91)

STRETCH-OUT:

Easy treading.
3 Waterworks.

Second Trimester—Week 15

SWIM POINTER:

- Timing your swims on the half-minute or 30-second mark in order to develop your timing abilities.

REMINDER:

Remember that every other swim will begin on the 30-second (half-minute) mark.

WARM-UP:

Bobbing in place for 30 seconds.
Rest 30 seconds.
Back flutter kick for 30 seconds.
Rest 30 seconds.
Standing scull for 30 seconds.
Rest 30 seconds.
Scissors kick for 30 seconds.
Rest 30 seconds.
Stretch legs and arms for 30 seconds.
Rest 30 seconds.

MAIN SWIM:

Level 1

Swim 2 × 50 yards on 1½ minutes (1:30).
Rest.
A 3-minute continuous swim.
Rest.
Swim 2 × 50 yards on 1½ minutes (1:30).

Level 2

Swim 3 × 50 yards on 1½ minutes (1:30).
Rest.
A 5-minute continuous swim.
Rest.
Swim 3 × 50 yards on 1½ minutes (1:30).

TRIMESTER 2

Level 3
    Swim 4 × 50 yards on 1½ minutes (1:30).
    Rest.
    A 7-minute continuous swim.
    Rest.
    Swim 4 × 50 yards on 1½ minutes (1:30).

STRETCH-OUT:

    5 Waterworks.

Second Trimester—Week 16

SWIM POINTERS:

• Using a cleansing breath before and after each exercise or swim.
• Focusing on your breaststroke.

REMINDERS:

The cleansing breath is an important basic breathing technique you'll use during your labor. Inhale slowly and fully through your nose, and then exhale by blowing all the air out through your mouth.
Rest between laps as needed.

WARM-UP:

Bobbing in place.
Rest.
Breaststroke kicking for 30 seconds.
1 cleansing breath, exhaling above water.
Heart-shaped breaststroke arm motion.
Standing in place for 30 seconds.
1 cleansing breath, exhaling below the water.
Leg stretches for 1 minute.
1 cleansing breath.

MAIN SWIM:

Level 1
Include a cleansing breath after each swim. Swim:
   1 × 25 yards
   1 × 50 yards
   1 × 100 yards
   1 × 50 yards
   1 × 25 yards.

Level 2
Include a cleansing breath after each swim. Swim:
   1 × 50 yards

TRIMESTER 2

    1 × 75 yards
    1 × 100 yards
    1 × 75 yards
    1 × 50 yards.

Level 3
Include a cleansing breath after each swim. Swim:
    1 × 25 yards
    1 × 75 yards
    1 × 100 yards
    1 × 200 yards
    1 × 100 yards
    1 × 75 yards
    1 × 25 yards.

STRETCH-OUT:

    Choose 5 Waterworks.

Second Trimester—Week 17

SWIM POINTERS:

· Try the variations of the sidestroke.
· After each lap include a cleansing breath.

REMINDERS:

There are 8 variations of the sidestroke, i.e.,
2 side motions—right and left
2 kicks—scissors and inverted scissors
2 arm motions—regular and top arm.
To practice on both sides, remember to face the same side of the pool for each lap.
Rest as needed between laps.

WARM-UP:

Bobbing in place.
A cleansing breath.
Wall scissors kick—both sides.
A cleansing breath.
Inverted scissors kick—both sides—on wall.
A cleansing breath.
Alternate overarm and regular sidestroke arm motions in place.
A cleansing breath.

MAIN SWIM:

Level 1

Swim 2 × 25 yards of sidestroke using the regular scissors kick (top leg forward).
Cleansing breath.
Swim 2 × 25 yards using the inverted scissors kick (top leg backward).
Cleansing breath.
Swim 2 × 25 yards using the regular scissors kick with the overarm variation.
Cleansing breath.

TRIMESTER 2 125

    Swim 2 × 25 yards using the inverted scissors kick with the overarm variation.

Level 2
    Swim 8 × 25 yards of sidestroke—use all variations (see Level 1).
    Cleansing breath.
    Swim 2 × 25 yards using the scissors kick (with a kickboard).
    Cleansing breath.
    Swim 1 × 100 yards—your choice.
    Cleansing breath.

Level 3
    Swim 8 × 25 yards of sidestroke—use all variations (see Level 1).
    Cleansing breath.
    Swim 1 × 100 yards—your choice.
    Cleansing breath.
    Swim 8 × 25 yards of sidestroke—all variations (see Level 1).

STRETCH-OUT:

    3 Waterworks.
    Easy flutter kicking.
    Treading water in place.

Second Trimester—Week 18

SWIM POINTERS:

- Sculling on back.
- Elementary backstroke.

REMINDERS:

Sculling is a figure eight motion.
In the elementary backstroke, both arms and legs move simultaneously.
Rest between laps as needed.

WARM-UP:

Scull in place and then walk backward.
Deepwater bobbing and breathing.
Sculling alone.
Breaststroke kick.
Combine both for treading.

MAIN SWIM:

Level 1

Scull 1 × 25 yards.
Cleansing breath.
Swim 1 × 50 yards of elementary backstroke.
Cleansing breath.
A 3-minute continuous swim.
Scull 1 × 25 yards.
Cleansing breath.
Swim 1 × 50 yards of elementary backstroke.

Level 2

Scull 1 × 25 yards.
Cleansing breath.
Swim 1 × 75 yards of elementary backstroke.
Cleansing breath.
Scull 1 × 25 yards.

TRIMESTER 2

    Cleansing breath.
    Swim 1 × 75 yards of elementary backstroke.

Level 3
    Scull 1 × 25 yards using your arms only.
    Cleansing breath.
    Swim 1 × 100 yards of elementary backstroke.
    Cleansing breath.
    Scull 1 × 25 yards.
    Cleansing breath.
    Swim 1 × 100 yards of elementary backstroke.

STRETCH-OUT:

    Choose 5 Waterworks.

Second Trimester—Week 19

SWIM POINTER:

· Timing your swims and rest periods at 15-second intervals in order to develop your timing abilities.

REMINDER:

Check your time after each swim and be ready to begin the next swim at the appropriate 15-second reading, i.e., 15, 30, 45, etc.

WARM-UP:

Bobbing for 15 seconds, rest 15 seconds, repeat.
Scissors kick on wall for 15 seconds, rest 15 seconds, repeat on other side 15 seconds.
Swim 2 easy laps—you choose the stroke(s).

MAIN SWIM:

Level 1
    Swim 4 × 25 yards of crawl stroke every 1:15, i.e.,
        1 × 25 yards (leave on 60)
        1 × 25 yards (leave on 15)
        1 × 25 yards (leave on 30)
        1 × 25 yards (leave on 45).
Rest.
A 5-minute swim—vary your strokes.

Level 2
    Swim 4 × 25 yards of crawl stroke every 45 seconds, i.e.,
        1 × 25 yards (leave on 60)
        1 × 25 yards (leave on 45)
        1 × 25 yards (leave on 30)
        1 × 25 yards (leave on 15).
A 5-minute continuous swim—vary your strokes.
Swim 4 × 25 yards of breaststroke or sidestroke every 1:15, i.e.,
        1 × 25 yards (leave on 60)
        1 × 25 yards (leave on 15)

TRIMESTER 2

    1 × 25 yards (leave on 30)
    1 × 25 yards (leave on 45).

Level 3

Swim 4 × 50 yards of crawl stroke every 1:15, i.e.,
    1 × 50 yards (leave on 60)
    1 × 50 yards (leave on 15)
    1 × 50 yards (leave on 30)
    1 × 50 yards (leave on 45).

Rest.

A 10-minute swim—vary your strokes.

Swim the breaststroke or the sidestroke 6 × 25 yards on 45 seconds, i.e.,
    1 × 25 yards (leave on 60)
    1 × 25 yards (leave on 45)
    1 × 25 yards (leave on 30)
    1 × 25 yards (leave on 15)
    1 × 25 yards (leave on 60)
    1 × 25 yards (leave on 45).

STRETCH-OUT:

Choose 5 Waterworks.

Second Trimester—Week 20

SWIM POINTERS:

- Inverted breaststroke.
- Windmill backstroke.
- Backstroke medley of strokes.

REMINDERS:

The inverted breaststoke is a combination of the breaststroke and the elementary backstroke.

The windmill backstroke is similar to the crawl's alternating arm motion.

WARM-UP:

Deepwater bobbing (i.e., bring your arms overhead with the palms up as you submerge, then press palms down to your sides to surface).
Easy flutter kick for 30 seconds.
Rest for 45 seconds.
Breaststroke kick for 30 seconds.
Rest for 45 seconds.
Windmill arm motion in chest-deep water.

MAIN SWIM:

Level 1

Swim 1 × 25 yards of inverted breaststroke.
Rest for 30 seconds.
Swim 1 × 25 yards of windmill backstroke.
Swim 100 yards—vary your strokes.
Swim 1 × 100 yards of backstroke medley with a rest (30 seconds) between sets:
    1 × 25 yards of sculling
    1 × 25 yards of elementary backstroke
    1 × 25 yards of inverted breaststroke
    1 × 25 yards of windmill backstroke

TRIMESTER 2

Level 2
    Swim 2 × 25 yards of inverted breaststroke.
    Swim 2 × 25 yards of windmill backstroke.
    Swim 200 yards—vary your strokes.
    Swim 1 × 100 yards of backstroke medley (see Level 1).
    Rest 30 seconds between sets.

Level 3
    Swim 1 × 50 yards of inverted breaststroke.
    Rest 30 seconds.
    Swim 1 × 50 yards of windmill backstroke.
    Swim 300 yards—vary your strokes.
    Swim 2 × 100 yards of backstroke medley (see Level 1).
    Rest 1 minute between sets.

STRETCH-OUT:
    Choose 3 Waterworks.
    Deepwater bobbing and treading.

Second Trimester—Week 21

SWIM POINTERS:

- Fartlek Conditioning (alternating an easy and moderate pace in a continuous swim).
- Combine 2 strokes, one at an easy pace and another at a moderate pace.

REMINDER:

Practice a newer stroke at an easy pace; swim the familiar stroke, e.g., the crawl, at a moderate pace.

WARM-UP:

Easy flutter kick for 30 seconds.
Moderate flutter kick for 30 seconds.
Easy scissors kick for 30 seconds.
Moderate breaststroke kick for 30 seconds.
Rest 30 seconds between kicks.

MAIN SWIM:

Level 1

Alternate 25- and 50-yard swims at an easy and moderate pace:
Swim 2 × 25 yards	Easy/Moderate
Rest for 30 seconds	
Swim 2 × 50 yards	Easy/Moderate
Rest for 30 seconds	
Swim 2 × 25 yards	Easy/Moderate

Level 2

Alternate 25-, 50-, and 75-yard swims (easy and moderate pace):
Swim 2 × 25 yards	Easy/Moderate
Rest	
Swim 2 × 50 yards	Easy/Moderate
Rest	
Swim 2 × 75 yards	Easy/Moderate
Rest	

TRIMESTER 2   133

    Swim 2 × 50 yards   Easy/Moderate
    Rest
    Swim 2 × 25 yards   Easy/Moderate

Level 3
    Alternate 50-, 75-, and 100-yard swims (easy and moderate pace):
    Swim 2 × 50 yards   Easy/Moderate
    Rest
    Swim 2 × 75 yards   Easy/Moderate
    Rest
    Swim 2 × 100 yards   Easy/Moderate
    Rest
    Swim 2 × 75 yards   Easy/Moderate
    Rest
    Swim 2 × 50 yards   Easy/Moderate

STRETCH-OUT:

    5 Waterworks.

Second Trimester—Week 22

SWIM POINTER:

• Medley of strokes with transitional turns.

REMINDERS:

Review stroke coordination cues.
Rest as needed between laps.

WARM-UP:

Medley of kicks on wall.
Try turn combinations: swim to wall with one stroke and change to another stroke on return lap, e.g., backstroke to breaststroke and breaststroke to crawl stroke.

MAIN SWIM:

Level 1
    Swim 1 × 100 yards of backstroke medley:
        Scull 1 × 25 yards
        Swim 1 × 25 yards of elementary backstroke
        Swim 1 × 25 yards of inverted breaststroke
        Swim 1 × 25 yards of windmill backstroke.
    Rest for 2 minutes.
    Swim 1 × 100 yards of medley of strokes:
        Swim 1 × 25 yards of sidestroke
        Swim 1 × 25 yards of backstroke
        Swim 1 × 25 yards of breaststroke
        Swim 1 × 25 yards of crawl stroke.

Level 2
    Swim 1 × 100 yards of medley of strokes (see Level 1).
    Rest.
    Swim 1 × 100 yards of backstroke medley (see Level 1).
    Rest.
    Swim 1 × 100 yards of reverse medley of strokes:
        Swim 1 × 25 yards of crawl stroke
        Swim 1 × 25 yards of breaststroke

TRIMESTER 2 135

      Swim 1 × 25 yards of backstroke
      Swim 1 × 25 yards of sidestroke.

Level 3

    Swim 1 × 200 yards of medley of strokes:
      Swim 1 × 50 yards of sidestroke
      Swim 1 × 50 yards of backstroke
      Swim 1 × 50 yards of breaststroke
      Swim 1 × 50 yards of crawl stroke.
Rest.
Swim 1 × 100 yards of backstroke medley (see Level 1).
Rest.
Swim 1 × 200 yards of reverse medley of strokes (see Level 2).

STRETCH-OUT:

    Choose 5 Waterworks.

Second Trimester—Week 23

SWIM POINTER:

· Timing your swims and rest periods at various intervals. This is good practice for timing labor contractions later.

REMINDER:

Make a mental note of the time your swim began and when it was completed. Start to plan ahead to begin your next swim on time.

WARM-UP:

Bob for 30 seconds.
Rest for 30 seconds.
Flutter kick for 20 seconds.
Rest for 40 seconds.
Scull for 45 seconds.
Rest for 15 seconds.
Tread water for 30 seconds.

MAIN SWIM:

Level 1
Swim 1 × 100 yards of medley of strokes (see Week 22).
Rest for 15 seconds in between laps.
Swim 1 × 25 yards of sidestroke.
Rest 15 seconds.
Swim 1 × 25 yards of backstroke.
Rest for 15 seconds.
Swim 1 × 25 yards of backstroke.
Rest 15 seconds.
Swim 1 × 25 yards of crawl stroke.
Swim 2 × 25 yards of crawl stroke on 1:10.

Level 2
Swim 1 × 100 yards of medley of strokes (see Week 22). Rest 15 seconds between laps.
Rest.
Swim 4 × 50 yards of crawl stroke on 2:15.

TRIMESTER 2

Rest.
Swim 2 × 25 yards on 50 seconds.

Level 3

Swim 1 × 100 yards of medley of strokes (see Week 22). Rest 15 seconds between laps. *6 dbs.*
Rest.
Swim 2 × 100 yards of crawl stroke on 2:30. *6 dbls / 6 dbls.*
Rest.
Swim 2 × 50 yards of crawl stroke on 1:45. *3 dbls / 3 dbls*
Rest.
Swim 4 × 25 yards of crawl stroke on 40 seconds. *1½ | 1½ | 1½ | 1½*

[margin: 7.91, 7.91, 6 dbs medley]

30 laps

STRETCH-OUT:

Choose 5 Waterworks.
Hold your stretch position in each exercise you choose for 30 seconds, and then rest for 30 seconds.

[handwritten notes:]
7.91. Medley
6 dbls — bkstrk. + crawl
6 dbls — sidestr + backstr.
12 dbls — medley
12 dbls. — medley

Second Trimester—Week 24

SWIM POINTERS:

- Kick-pull-swim variations.
- Experiment with fins, kickboard, paddles, and pull buoys, etc.

REMINDERS:

Using available swim equipment is optional, but it may be helpful and it may enhance your workout.
Try them, maybe you'll like them!

WARM-UP:

Wall flutter kick—fins optional.
Standing arm stroke—paddles optional.
Press the kickboard down toward your knees and slowly let it up.
Repeat 10 times.

MAIN SWIM:

Level 1

Swim 4 × 50 yards using a stroke and the equipment of your choice:
  Swim 1 × 50 yards
  Pull 1 × 50 yards
  Kick 1 × 50 yards
  Swim 1 × 50 yards.
Rest between 50-yard swims.

Level 2

Pull-Kick-Swim 1 × 150 yards (stroke and equipment are your choice):
  Pull 1 × 50 yards
  Kick 1 × 50 yards
  Swim 1 × 50 yards.
Rest.
Swim 1 × 100 yards of medley of strokes (see Week 22).
Rest.
Pull-Kick-Swim 1 × 150 yards.

TRIMESTER 2

Level 3

Pull-Kick-Swim 1 × 300 yards (stroke and equipment are your choice):
- Pull 1 × 100 yards   6 dbl
- Kick 1 × 100 yards   6 dbl
- Swim 1 × 100 yards.   6 dbs

Rest.
Swim 1 × 100 yards of medley of strokes (see Week 22). 6 dbs.
Rest.
Pull-Kick-Swim 1 × 150 yards:
- Pull 1 × 50 yards   3 dbs
- Kick 1 × 50 yards   3 dbs   33 lengths
- Swim 1 × 50 yards.   3 dbs

STRETCH-OUT:

Alternately stretch your arms and your legs with different Waterworks exercises.

15/7/91 Will try but need to buy a kickboard/pull buoy & paw
         Did so!
18/7/91 And again!
20/7/91   "   "

CHARTING YOUR SWIMS: PERSONAL SWIM LOG

TRIMESTER 2

Week/Date	Pool Location and Length	Warm-Up	Main Swim	Stretch-Out	Total Time/Distance of Workout	Weight	Comments
13 1/5/91 10/5/91	Fulham Aquaderm	stretches	15m - 18 length	stretches	25-30min	10/2	Difficult today
"	"	"	18 length + 2 con't	"	25min	11 69kg	OK
14 13/5/91 15/5/91	Stephanie listed	N5+o c5! 25/35 /25 kicks	Fastest 40m's 6 min rest	Ease into stretches	25 min 40 min	?	Not posi-a awd. Very hard - esp. stop/start
15 18/5/91	Fulham	OK	19 min	OK	30 min	10/11	Breathing today
16 20/5/91 26/5/91	Fulham Stephanie WBA	OK OK	20-25 min 21 min	OK OK	30 min 3.5 min	11/1 "	Almost coal head OK - ?
17 2/6/92	Fulham	OK	21 min	OK	25 min	11 - Today	OK - breakache ribs painful
" 4.6.96	Stephanie	OK	20 min	OK	20 min	?	OK
18 6.6.91	Fitness Complex-Nore	OK	(general) 20 min	OK	20 min	?	Ribs ache bad - trying to keep stretched
19 12.6.91 14 9/6 —	Stephanie "	OK OK	20 min 25 min	"	25 min 30 min	? ?	OK - eased ribs ache Feeling good
20 13 6 9/am 16.6.91	" "	OK OK	25 mins 25 min	2 legs 3 kicks "	30 min	?	Normal travel Breathing difficult
21 23.6. 9 am 27.6. 91am	" "	OK OK	" "	" "	25 min	72.8	Ribs/hipoint Sok
22 30.6.91 3.7.91	Good Stuttle Classen	"	25 min	"	25 min	72.9	Fine
23 7.7.91 10.7.91	Stephanie "	" "	" "	2 laps 3 kicks 6 IPS mainly	" "	74.4 73.4	Fine "
24 15.7.91 22.7.91	" "	" "	25 min "	" "	" "	73.8 73.8	" "

20

Trimester 3

In your third trimester swimming program, you'll continue to increase your fitness, strength, and flexibility, and you'll practice the Waterworks exercises more related to the exercises taught in many prepared childbirth programs. During your third trimester, you'll ease up so that your workouts become less demanding than they were during your first and second trimesters, you'll reduce your main swim by up to 10 minutes, and you'll increase your warm-up and stretch-out time so that each phase takes about 10 minutes. The third trimester program ends at your thirty-sixth week, although your pregnancy will last approximately 40 weeks. Should you wish to continue swimming past the thirty-sixth week, continue with that week's program. Check with your doctor to determine how far into your pregnancy you may continue your swimming program, and keep him or her informed of your progress.

Breathing exercises are especially important during your third trimester. Concentrate on full inhalation and exhalation, and practice breathing patterns combined with effleurage.

Take one day at a time during your third trimester, and adjust each swimming session to your comfort. Avoid strokes that feel uncomfortable. Spend extra time relaxing after your swim.

During your third trimester, you may experience the return of some of the discomforts of the first trimester for different reasons. As the baby drops into the pelvis, you may experience increased frequency of urination, caused by pressure on the bladder. You may also become fatigued more easily because of your extra bulk and weight.

The third trimester swimming program offers:
- Review of cleansing breath.
- Introduction to prepared childbirth breathing exercises used during labor and delivery.
- Introduction to variations of prepared childbirth exercises, such as the effleurage, tailor sit, Kegel, focal concentration, and pelvic rock.
- Increased length of warm-up and stretch-out time.
- Pull-swim combination.
- Sidestroke variations.
- Relaxation, comfort, floating and recreation in the water.

Third Trimester—Week 25

SWIM POINTER:

- Stroke-count for the breaststroke—this helps to improve your concentration while swimming.

REMINDER:

Focus on a long, relaxed glide in your stroke.

WARM-UP:

Choose 5 Waterworks, one from each of the following categories:
  Breathing
  Upper body
  Middle body
  Lower body
  Total body

MAIN SWIM:

Level 1
  Swim 1 × 25 yards using the breaststroke stroke count.
  Swim 1 × 50 yards—choose any stroke.
  Rest.
  Swim 1 × 25 yards using the breaststroke stroke count.
  Swim 1 × 50 yards—choose any stroke.
  Rest.
  Swim 1 × 25 yards using the breaststroke stroke count.
  Swim 1 × 50 yards—choose any stroke.
  Rest.
  Swim 1 × 25 yards using the breaststroke stroke count.

Level 2
  Swim 1 × 25 yards using the breaststroke stroke count.
  Swim 1 × 100 yards—choose any stroke.
  Rest.
  Swim 1 × 25 yards using the breaststroke stroke count.
  Swim 1 × 100 yards—choose any stroke.

Rest.
Swim 1 × 25 yards using the breaststroke stroke count.

Level 3

Swim 1 × 50 yards using the breaststroke stroke count.
Swim 1 × 100 yards—choose any stroke.
Rest.
Swim 1 × 50 yards using the breaststroke stroke count.
Swim 1 × 100 yards—choose any stroke.
Rest.
Swim 1 × 50 yards using the breaststroke stroke count.
Swim 1 × 100 yards—choose any stroke.
Rest.
Swim 1 × 50 yards using the breaststroke stroke count.

STRETCH-OUT:

In the floating with safe recovery Waterworks position, alternately stretch and relax.
Easy treading and bobbing.
Try some new Waterworks.

Third Trimester—Week 26

SWIM POINTERS:

• Coordinate your cleansing breath into your swim session.
• 3-stroke medley (in prone, side, and back positions).

REMINDERS:

For your cleansing breath, inhale through your nose and exhale through your mouth.
Choose your medley strokes from the following:
- Prone—crawl or breaststroke
- Side—sidestroke, either side, either kick, with regular or overarm motion
- Back—elementary, inverted, or windmill backstroke.

WARM-UP:

Choose 5 Waterworks.
Between each of the Waterworks exercises, do 1 cleansing breath.

MAIN SWIM:

Level 1
Swim 1 × 75 yards of medley of strokes:
    1 × 25 yards in prone position
    1 × 25 yards in side position
    1 × 25 yards in back position.
Rest. Cleansing breath.
Swim 1 × 75 yards of medley of strokes.

Level 2
Swim 1 × 75 yards of medley of strokes:
    1 × 25 yards in prone position
    1 × 25 yards in side position
    1 × 25 yards in back position.
Rest. Cleansing breath.
Swim 1 × 150 yards of medley of strokes:
    1 × 50 yards in prone position

1 × 50 yards in side position
1 × 50 yards in back position.
Rest. Cleansing breath.
Swim 1 × 75 yards of medley of strokes.

Level 3

Swim 1 × 150 yards of medley of strokes:
1 × 50 yards in prone position
1 × 50 yards in side position
1 × 50 yards in back position.
Rest. Cleansing breath.
Swim 1 × 75 yards of medley of strokes:
1 × 25 yards in prone position
1 × 25 yards in side position
1 × 25 yards in back position.
Rest. Cleansing breath.

STRETCH-OUT:

Choose any Waterworks exercises.
Do 1 cleansing breath between exercises.

Third Trimester—Week 27

SWIM POINTERS:

- Coordinate your effleurage into your swim session.
- Pull-swim combination in a pyramid.

REMINDER:

Focus on your effleurage between Waterworks and during your rest periods. Choose the stroke(s) that are most comfortable.

WARM-UP:

Choose 5 Waterworks; in between, practice your effleurage.

MAIN SWIM:

Level 1
    Pull 1 × 25 yards
    Swim 1 × 25 yards
    Rest. Effleurage.
    Pull 1 × 50 yards
    Swim 1 × 50 yards
    Rest. Effleurage.
    Pull 1 × 25 yards
    Swim 1 × 25 yards

Level 2
    Pull 1 × 25 yards
    Swim 1 × 25 yards
    Rest. Effleurage.
    Pull 1 × 50 yards
    Swim 1 × 50 yards
    Rest. Effleurage.
    Pull 1 × 75 yards
    Swim 1 × 75 yards

Level 3

Pull 1 × 25 yards
Swim 1 × 25 yards
Rest. Effleurage.
Pull 1 × 50 yards
Swim 1 × 50 yards
Rest. Effleurage.
Pull 1 × 75 yards
Swim 1 × 75 yards
Rest. Effleurage.
Pull 1 × 50 yards
Swim 1 × 50 yards
Rest. Effleurage.
Pull 1 × 25 yards
Swim 1 × 25 yards

STRETCH-OUT:

Easy treading in place.
Effleurage.
Float and stretch on your back.

Third Trimester—Week 28

SWIM POINTER:

- Focus on coordinating your exhalation with the glide phase of the breaststroke, sidestroke, elementary backstroke, or inverted breaststroke.

REMINDERS:

Exhale completely during the glide phase.
Try to concentrate and relax completely during your glide.
Practice your cleansing breath and effleurage.

WARM-UP:

Choose 2 Waterworks.
Practice walking sidestroke and breaststroke arm motions in place.
Practice the elementary backstroke arm motion (underwater recovery) in place.

MAIN SWIM:

Level 1
Swim 1 × 75 yards using the breaststroke.
Rest.
Swim 1 × 75 yards using the sidestroke.
Rest.
Swim 1 × 75 yards using the elementary backstroke or inverted breaststroke.

Level 2
Swim 1 × 75 yards using the breaststroke.
Rest.
Swim 1 × 150 yards—choose any stroke.
Rest.
Swim 1 × 75 yards using the backstroke or sidestroke.

Level 3
Swim 1 × 75 yards using the breaststroke.
Rest.

Swim 1 × 150 yards using the sidestroke.
Rest.
Swim 1 × 150 yards using the elementary backstroke or inverted breaststroke.
Rest.
Swim 1 × 75 yards—choose any stroke.

STRETCH-OUT:

2 Waterworks:
Floating with safe recovery Waterworks.
Pendulum body swing Waterworks (prone to supine position).
Effleurage and cleansing breath.

TRIMESTER 3   151

Third Trimester—Week 29

SWIM POINTER:

· Gradual increase in the length of your warm-up and your stretch-out from 5 minutes to 6 minutes.

REMINDERS:

To maintain your total workout time, your main swim time will be decreased accordingly.

Practice your cleansing breath and effleurage during your rest periods.

WARM-UP:

Increase your time by choosing 6 Waterworks and do each one for approximately 1 minute.

MAIN SWIM:

Level 1
Swim 3 minutes continuously.
Rest for 2 minutes.
Swim for 3 minutes continuously.

Level 2
Swim 5 minutes continuously.
Rest for 3 minutes.
Swim 5 minutes continuously.

Level 3
Swim 10 minutes continuously.
Rest for 3 minutes.
Swim 5 minutes continuously.

STRETCH-OUT:

Increase your stretch-out time.
Use stationary pool structures to help you stretch-out, e.g., the ladder, the steps, the wall, or the railing.

Third Trimester—Week 30

SWIM POINTER:

· Focus on reaching and stretching out while you are swimming.

REMINDERS:

Increase warm-up and stretch-out time to 7 minutes each.
Emphasize your reach, stretch, and glide.
Do effleurage and cleansing breaths simultaneously between Waterworks and swims.

WARM-UP:

Increase your time by choosing 7 Waterworks and do each one for approximately 1 minute.
Practice cleansing breaths between Waterworks.

MAIN SWIM:

Level 1
   Swim 3 × 50 yards using the crawl stroke or any stroke you choose.
   Rest between 50-yard swims.

Level 2
   Swim 3 × 100 yards using the crawl stroke or any stroke you choose.
   Rest between 100-yard swims.

Level 3
   Swim 3 × 100 yards using the crawl or your choice of strokes.
   Rest between 100-yard swims.
   Swim 2 × 50 yards using any stroke.
   Rest between 50-yard swims.

STRETCH-OUT:

Increase your stretch-out time to 7 minutes.
Choose 7 Waterworks, and review practicing cleansing breaths between each.

Third Trimester—Week 31

SWIM POINTER:

- Focus on sidestroke variations.

REMINDERS:

Use different sidestroke variations during each lap, and always face the same side of the pool.
Increase your warm-up and stretch-out time to 8 minutes each.

WARM-UP:

Increase your warm-up to 8 minutes.
Practice the cleansing breath in between Waterworks.

MAIN SWIM:

Level 1
   Swim 1 × 50 yards using the sidestroke.
   Rest.
   Swim 1 × 50 yards using the sidestroke.

Level 2
   Swim 1 × 50 yards using the sidestroke.
   Rest.
   Swim 1 × 50 yards using the sidestroke.
   Swim 1 × 50 yards—choose any backstroke variation.
   Swim 2 × 50 yards using the sidestroke.

Level 3
   Swim 2 × 50 yards using the sidestroke.
   Swim 1 × 100 yards—choose any backstroke variation.
   Rest.
   Swim 2 × 50 yards using the sidestroke.
   Swim 1 × 100 yards—your choice of stroke.

STRETCH-OUT:

Increase your stretch-out time to 8 minutes.
Practice your cleansing breath between Waterworks exercises.

Third Trimester—Week 32

SWIM POINTER:

· Focus on deep chest breathing pattern, used in early labor (6 to 9 breaths per minute).

REMINDER:

Maintain warm-up and stretch-out time for a maximum of 10 minutes each.

WARM-UP:

Increase Waterworks time to 9 to 10 minutes.
Include front to back water push Waterworks.
Begin deep chest breathing.

MAIN SWIM:

Level 1
Lap swimming optional.

Level 2
5 minutes of easy lap swimming.
Rest at the midpoint of your swim.

Level 3
10 minutes of easy lap swimming. Vary strokes.
Rest at the midpoint of your swim.

STRETCH-OUT:

Increase Waterworks time to 9 or 10 minutes.
Include water Kegel Waterworks.
Practice deep chest breathing.

Third Trimester—Week 33

SWIM POINTER:

- Focus on shallow upper chest breathing pattern used during the first stage of active labor.

REMINDERS:

Review deep chest breathing (6 to 9 breaths per minute).
Maintain warm-up and stretch-out times for a maximum of 10 minutes each.

WARM-UP:

Maintain 9 to 10 minutes of Waterworks.
Include treading and bobbing.
Practice shallow upper chest breathing pattern.

MAIN SWIM:

Level 1
Brief lap swimming is optional.

Level 2
5 minutes of easy lap swimming.
Rest when needed.

Level 3
10 minutes of easy lap swimming.
Rest when needed.

STRETCH-OUT:

Maintain 9 to 10 minutes of Waterworks.
Hang ten Waterworks.
Review deep chest and shallow upper chest breathing patterns for first stage of labor.

Third Trimester—Week 34

SWIM POINTERS:

- Focus on transition breathing, which helps you overcome the urge to push.
- (This includes 4 to 6 rapid chest breaths followed by a strong exhalation.)

REMINDER:

Review previous breathing patterns in sequence: early, active, and transition.

WARM-UP:

Maintain 9 to 10 minutes of Waterworks.
Include pelvic rock for middle body Waterworks.
Practice transition breathing.

MAIN SWIM:

Level 1
Brief lap swimming is optional.

Level 2
5 minutes of easy lap swimming.
Rest at least twice.

Level 3
10 minutes of easy lap swimming.
Rest at least once.

STRETCH-OUT:

Maintain 9 to 10 minutes of Waterworks.
Wall walk Waterworks and Lamaze tailor sit Waterworks.
Review breathing patterns in sequence.

Third Trimester—Week 35

SWIM POINTER:

- Focus on second stage pushing to birth breathing pattern. (This entails 2 quick cleansing breaths; on the third breath, hold and push. Then breathe in and repeat.)

REMINDER:

Review all breathing patterns used during labor and delivery: early, active, transition, pushing, and afterbirth (third stage or afterbirth breathing is similar to pushing).

WARM-UP:

Maintain 9 to 10 minutes of Waterworks.
Include pushing abdominal Waterworks.
Practice second stage pushing breathing pattern.

MAIN SWIM:

Level 1
Brief lap swim is optional.

Level 2
5 minutes of easy lap swimming.
Rest whenever needed.

Level 3
10 minutes of easy lap swimming.
Rest whenever needed.

STRETCH-OUT:

Maintain 9 to 10 minutes of Waterworks.
Posture check Waterworks.
Review all breathing patterns used during labor and delivery.

Third Trimester—Week 36

SWIM POINTERS:

- Review and focus on all breathing exercises used during labor and delivery.
- Focus on total body relaxation in the water.

REMINDERS:

Since this is your last swim session, check with your doctor to see if you should stop or if you can continue your swim program until you give birth.

If you continue, remember to review your breathing and specific suggested Waterworks.

Keep this swimming book handy. See you after your baby's birth for your postpartum program.

WARM-UP:

Maintain 9 to 10 minutes of Waterworks.
Total body focal relaxation Waterworks.
Review all 5 breathing techniques.

MAIN SWIM:

Level 1
Brief lap swimming is optional.

Level 2
5 minutes of easy lap swimming.
Rest whenever needed.

Level 3
10 minutes of easy lap swimming.
Rest whenever needed.

STRETCH-OUT:

Maintain 9 to 10 minutes of Waterworks.
Floating with safe recovery Waterworks.
Review all breathing techniques.

CHARTING YOUR SWIMS: PERSONAL SWIM LOG

TRIMESTER 3

Week/Date	Pool Location and Length	Warm-Up	Main Swim	Stretch-Out	Total Time/ Distance of Workout	Weight	Comments
25 22/7, 28/7	Stephanie 9yd	Stretch	22 min	"	25 min	74.3	ok, ok
26 30/7, 2/8	HSRdy Hm Dog, Shepton 5yd	"	22 min, 20 min	"	2 hr	74.3	Lost breath – fine
27 4/8, 7/8	"	Swim	25 min, 23 min	Effleurage	25 min, 45 min	—	ok
28 11/8, 15/8	"	"	"	"	"	73.2	ok - contractions
29 18/8, 25/8	"	"	23 min	"	"	75.7, 76.1	ok, ok
30 1/9	Fulham Stephanie	"	"	"	"	76.	ok
31 5/9, 8/9	"	"	20 min, 20 min 27 db.	"	22 min, 20 min	74.5	ok
32 12/9, 15/9	"	"	"	"	"	"	"
33 29/9	"	"	"	"	"	"	"
34 2/9, 3/10	Fulham Stephanie	"	"	"	"	?	"
35 6/10, 10/10	"	"	"	"	"	78 kg	"
36 13/10, 17/10	"	"	"	"	"	"	"

37 20/10
38 24/10
39 27/11

75/lds (boy)

Sophie born 5.11.91 3.55pm !!

IV

Postpartum Program

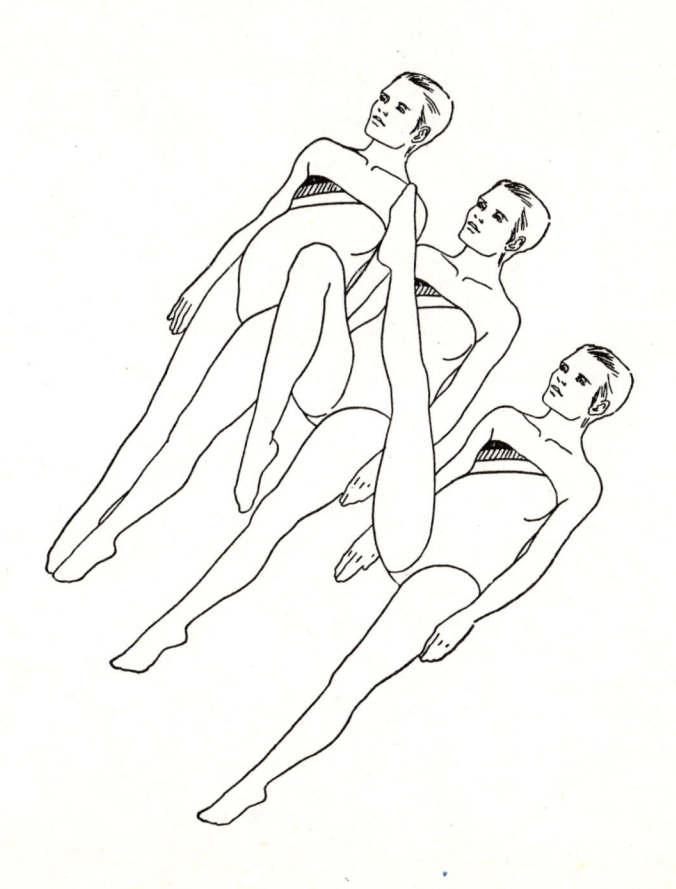

21

Introduction

You've just experienced one of humankind's most remarkable experiences: giving birth. The object of the book has been to prepare your body, through swimming, for labor and delivery. Most probably, your efforts were rewarded and the conditioning of your body was a great help to you during delivery. This conditioning should also help you recover quicker from delivery.

You either had a vaginal delivery or a Cesarean section delivery (C-section). If you had a vaginal, you probably had an episiotomy to make the delivery easier on you. If you had a C-section, you may have had a bikini incision or a navel to pubic bone incision; in either case, you had abdominal surgery and your muscles need time to heal. Lochia, a vaginal discharge, is a natural drainage of the uterus following delivery which lasts approximately six weeks. Wait until the discharge has ceased before beginning the program. And whether you are recovering from a vaginal delivery or a C-section delivery, check with your doctor before resuming this or any other exercise program. After you've received the doctor's okay, you're ready to take the plunge.

What follows is a swim exercise program for use during your postpartum period which:

• is a twelve-week progressive swim program with suggested workouts, and
• will include an introduction to:
 — synchronized swimming (water ballet)

– diving
– the butterfly stroke

During this part of the program, you will learn and use skills progressively, and you'll be moving from easy workouts to more difficult workouts. The program lasts twelve weeks, and if you follow it, you'll be prepared to go on to a more rigorous swimming program.

The postpartum program is similar to the pregnancy program in that each exercise session will commence with a five-minute warm-up, proceed to a main swim of twenty to thirty minutes, and finish with a five-minute stretch-out. In addition, there are three levels of main swim exercises from which you select, depending on your fitness level and recovery from delivery. Don't hesitate to change from level to level in the main swim—let your health and fitness be your guide and listen to your body.

An introduction to synchronized swimming (water ballet) is included (see chapter 23), because it is a terrific conditioner, as well as a great deal of fun. It employs all the muscles of the body, develops grace and coordination, and is a terrific aerobic exercise. It also helps to burn calories. As you become more fit and more skilled, you'll be able to progress from water ballet to synchronized swimming exercises which utilize more challenging movements and patterns. What a great way to expand your swimming repertoire.

Let the following tips guide you in your postpartum program:

- You must have your doctor's approval.
- You must be completely healed from delivery before commencing your exercise program. Your doctor will advise you when the healing process is complete.
- To regain your prepregnancy figure, pay special attention to the following areas:
    – buttocks
    – upper, outer, and inner thighs
    – abdomen, chest, and waist.
- Don't be discouraged if you tire easily.
- You've assumed a new role as mother, and you'll have to adjust other aspects of your life to it. This may take some time, but *don't* get discouraged.
- It may take you a year to return to your prepregnancy figure and weight. This is a slow process, but in the long run, it is better to move gradually toward your former figure and weight than crash-diet in order to lose the weight all at once.

INTRODUCTION 165

- Your uterus will not return to its prepregnancy state, and your cervix will be enlarged, but this in no way will affect your appearance.
- Swimming is good for the inner you and the outer you. Return to the basics and work your way up.
- Try to set aside a specific amount of time to devote to your swimming. Try to have your spouse join you—the baby will join you later.
- The timing of your return to swimming is up to you.
- If you find that you're having some difficulty swimming, increase the time you spend for the warm-up and the stretch-out. You may have to give yourself a "mental shove" but don't give up—the benefits of swimming are worth the extra effort.
- When you return to the pool, I recommend that you try to start at the third level of the first trimester. However, if you need to start at an easier level, do so.
- Explore other forms of swimming activity.

22

Twelve-Week Progressive Swim Program

Postpartum Workouts—Week 1

SWIM POINTER:

To get back into a swim routine and to enjoy the relaxing benefits of the water.

REMINDERS:

Are you ready?
Check with your doctor for the "go ahead" to resume your swims.
Listen to your body.

WARM-UP:

Bobbing and breathing.
Medley of Waterworks kicking exercises.
Choose 3 other Waterworks and rest after each one.

MAIN SWIM:

Level 1
Swim for 10 minutes using a variety of strokes.
Rest as needed.

Level 2
    Swim 15 minutes using a variety of strokes.
    Rest as needed.
Level 3
    Swim 20 minutes using a variety of strokes.
    Rest as needed.

STRETCH-OUT:

    Hang ten Waterworks exercise.
    Choose 3 other Waterworks.
    Treading and floating.

Postpartum Workouts—Week 2

SWIM POINTERS:

- An introduction to synchronized swimming.
- Reviewing sculling.
- Using the layout position and the log roll.

REMINDER:

Refer to the swimming skills in chapter 23. They're great for toning your body now.

WARM-UP:

Bobbing and breathing.
Choose 3 Waterworks.
Easy treading.

MAIN SWIM:

Level 1
Swim for 3 minutes continuously.
Rest.
Scull 1 × 25 yards using the elementary backstroke.
Rest.
From your back layout position, try log rolls to the right and to the left—use the flutter kick with fins.

Level 2
Swim for 5 minutes continuously.
Rest.
Scull 1 × 25 yards.
Rest.
1 × 25 yards elementary backstroke.
From your back layout position, try log rolls to the right and left—use the flutter kick with fins.

Level 3
Swim for 10 minutes continuously, varying your strokes and resting as needed.
Rest.

Scull 1 × 25 yards.
Rest.
Scull 1 × 25 yards.
From the back layout position, try your log rolls:
>to the right and to the left;
>with flutter kick with fins;
>two rolls continuously.

STRETCH-OUT:

Treading and floating.
3 Waterworks.
Log roll.

Postpartum Workouts—Week 3

SWIM POINTERS:

- Review backstroke medley skills.
- Practice tuck position.
- Include sculling, elementary backstroke, inverted breaststroke, and windmill backstroke.

REMINDERS:

Try rotating your shoulders when doing the windmill backstroke.
Remember that the sit-up position is similar to your tuck position.

WARM-UP:

Bobbing and breathing.
Modified sit-ups Waterworks.
Choose 3 Waterworks exercises.

MAIN SWIM:

Level 1
   5-minute swim—include all backstrokes.
   Rest.
   1 × 25 yards sculling in tuck position.
   Rest.
   1 × 50 yards backstroke your choice (use a half turn in tuck position at the wall).
   Rest.
   1 × 25 yards sculling in tuck position.
   Rest.
   Practice tuck turns to the right and left.

Level 2
   1 × 25 yards sculling.
   Rest.
   1 × 25 yards sculling.
   Rest.
   7-minute continuous swim. Alternate every other lap on your back.

Rest.
Practice tuck turns to the right and left.
Rest.
Backstroke medley:
- 1 × 25 yards sculling
- 1 × 25 yards elementary backstroke
- 1 × 25 yards inverted breaststroke
- 1 × 25 yards windmill backstroke.

Level 3

1 × 25 yards sculling. Begin in tuck position.
Rest.
1 × 50 yards backstroke.
Rest.
1 × 25 yards sculling. Begin in tuck position.
10-minute continuous swim. Swim every other lap on your back.
Rest.
Practice tuck turns to right and left.
1 × 100 yards backstroke medley:
- 1 × 25 yards sculling
- 1 × 25 yards elementary backstroke
- 1 × 25 yards inverted breaststroke
- 1 × 25 yards backstroke.

STRETCH-OUT:

Review log rolls.
Treading and floating.
Easy bobbing.

Postpartum Workouts—Week 4

SWIM POINTERS:

- Review variations of sidestroke.
- Practice marlin turn.

REMINDER:

There are 8 different variations of sidestroke (2 arm, 2 leg, on either side).

WARM-UP:

Bobbing and breathing.
Medley of pulls Waterworks.
Review log roll.

MAIN SWIM:

Level 1

7-minute continuous swim, including sidestroke variations.
Rest.
1 × 50 yards backstroke your choice.
Practice marlin turns to the right and left.

Level 2

10-minute continuous swim, include sidestroke variations.
Rest.
1 × 50 yards backstroke your choice.
Practice marlin turns to the right and left.

Level 3

12-minute continuous swim, include sidestroke variations.
Rest.
1 × 100 yards backstroke medley:
    1 × 25 yards sculling
    1 × 25 yards elementary backstroke
    1 × 25 yards inverted breaststroke
    1 × 25 yards windmill backstroke.
Practice marlin turns to the right and left.

STRETCH-OUT:

    Review tuck turn and log roll.
    Treading and floating.
    Waterworks exercises.

Postpartum Workouts—Week 5

SWIM POINTERS:

- Butterfly stroke skills (double overarm backstroke).
- Clam.
- Resume interval swims.

REMINDERS:

Remember, the butterfly arm motion is similar to the crawl S-pull, except that your arms move forward simultaneously in the butterfly, rather than alternately, as in the crawl.

When doing the clam, try to keep legs straight.

WARM-UP:

Bobbing and breathing.
Arm circles Waterworks.
Practice the clam.

MAIN SWIM:

Level 1

1 × 25 yards double overarm backstroke.
Rest.
1 × 25 yards easy crawl.
3 × 25 yards your choice. Vary your strokes. Rest 30 seconds between swims.
Rest.
1 × 50 yards crawl stroke, timed swim.

Level 2

1 × 25 yards double overarm backstroke.
1 × 25 yards easy crawl.
Rest.
3 × 100 yards. Vary your strokes. Rest 30 seconds between swims.
Rest.
1 × 50 yards crawl stroke, timed swim.

Level 3
    1 × 25 yards double overarm backstroke.
    1 × 25 yards easy crawl.
    Rest.
    3 × 150 yards. Vary your strokes. Rest 30 seconds between swims.
    Rest.
    1 × 50 yards crawl stroke, timed swim.

STRETCH-OUT:

    Treading and floating.
    Practice the clam.
    Waterworks exercises.

Postpartum Workouts—Week 6

SWIM POINTERS:

- Dolphin kick for butterfly stroke.
- Shark circle.
- Pyramid swim.

REMINDERS:

Keep your legs moving together for the dolphin kick.
Combine the crawl arm motion with the dolphin kick.

WARM-UP:

Bobbing and breathing.
Pelvic rock Waterworks.
Hula-Hoop hip rotation Waterworks.
Shark circle to the left and right.

MAIN SWIM:

Level 1
    1 × 25 yards dolphin kick.
    Rest.
    1 × 25 yards crawl stroke with dolphin kick.
    Pyramid swim—rest 30 seconds between swims:
        1 × 25 yards
        1 × 50 yards
        1 × 100 yards
        1 × 50 yards
        1 × 25 yards.

Level 2
    1 × 25 yards dolphin kick.
    Rest.
    1 × 25 yards crawl stroke with dolphin kick.
    Pyramid swim—rest 30 seconds between swims:
        1 × 50 yards
        1 × 75 yards

      1 × 100 yards
      1 × 75 yards
      1 × 50 yards.
Rest.
1 × 25 yards dolphin kick.
1 × 25 yards crawl stroke with dolphin kick.

Level 3
1 × 25 yards dolphin kick.
Rest.
1 × 25 yards crawl stroke with dolphin kick.
Pyramid swim—rest 30 seconds between swims:
      1 × 50 yards
      1 × 100 yards
      1 × 150 yards
      1 × 100 yards
      1 × 50 yards.
Rest.
1 × 25 yards dolphin kick.
1 × 25 yards crawl stroke with dolphin kick.

STRETCH-OUT:

Treading and floating.
Shark circle to the right and left.
Review marlin turn, tuck turn and log roll.

Postpartum Workouts—Week 7

SWIM POINTERS:

- Butterfly arm motion.
- Kick-pull-swim set.
- Dolphin circle.

REMINDER:

Combine the butterfly arm motion with the flutter kick.

SAFETY TIP:

Be certain to practice the dolphin circle in at least 6 feet of water.
To get you started, begin the dolphin circle by pushing off from the wall on your back.

WARM-UP:

Review the shark circle.
Practice any total body Waterworks and include arm circles.
Practice the dolphin circle.

MAIN SWIM:

Level 1
    1 × 75 yards kick-pull-swim butterfly:
        1 × 25 yards dolphin kick
        1 × 25 yards butterfly arm motion
        1 × 25 yards combine butterfly arm motion with flutter, frog, or dolphin kick.
Rest.
    1 × 75 yards kick-pull-swim crawl stroke:
        1 × 25 yards flutter kick
        1 × 25 yards crawl arm motion
        1 × 25 yards crawl stroke.
Rest.
    1 × 75 yards kick-pull-swim—choice of stroke.
    1 × 25 yards easy swim.

Level 2

1 × 75 yards kick-pull-swim butterfly:
    1 × 25 yards dolphin kick
    1 × 25 yards butterfly arm motion
    1 × 25 yards combine butterfly arm motion with flutter, breaststroke, or dolphin kick.

Rest.

1 × 150 yards kick-pull-swim crawl stroke:
    1 × 50 yards flutter kick
    1 × 50 yards crawl arm pull
    1 × 50 yards crawl stroke.

Rest.

1 × 75 yards kick-pull-swim—choice of stroke.
1 × 50 yards easy swim.

Level 3

1 × 75 yards kick-pull-swim butterfly:
    1 × 25 yards dolphin kick
    1 × 25 yards butterfly arm pull
    1 × 25 yards combine butterfly arm pull with flutter, frog, or dolphin kick.

Rest.

1 × 225 yards kick-pull-swim crawl stroke:
    1 × 75 yards flutter kick
    1 × 75 yards crawl arm pull
    1 × 75 yards crawl stroke.

Rest.

1 × 150 yards kick-pull-swim—choice of stroke.
1 × 50 yards easy swim.

STRETCH-OUT:

Hang ten Waterworks.
Treading and floating.
Dolphin circle.
Easy sculling.

Postpartum Workouts—Week 8

SWIM POINTERS:

- Butterfly with dolphin kick.
- Individual medley of swim strokes.
- Bent knee marching step position.

REMINDERS:

The individual medley consists of butterfly, backstroke, breaststroke, and crawl.

Practice the bent knee marching step position by first facing the wall and resting your foot on the edge, step, or ladder for support. Keep your leg straight.

WARM-UP:

Aqua jogging Waterworks, bringing knees up high.
Bent knee position with wall support.
Modified sit-ups Waterworks.
Medley of pulls Waterworks.

MAIN SWIM:

Level 1
    1 × 100 yards individual medley:
        1 × 25 yards butterfly
        1 × 25 yards backstroke your choice
        1 × 25 yards breaststroke
        1 × 25 yards crawl stroke.
  Rest.
    1 × 100 yards stroke choice.
  Rest.
    1 × 100 yards individual medley.

Level 2
    1 × 100 yards individual medley:
        1 × 25 yards butterfly
        1 × 25 yards backstroke your choice

1 × 25 yards breaststroke
1 × 25 yards crawl stroke.
Rest.
1 × 200 yards stroke choice.
Rest.
1 × 100 yards individual medley.

Level 3
1 × 100 yards individual medley:
1 × 25 yards butterfly
1 × 25 yards backstroke
1 × 25 yards breaststroke
1 × 25 yards crawl stroke.
Rest.
1 × 200 yards stroke choice.
Rest.
1 × 100 yards individual medley.
Rest.
1 × 200 yards stroke choice.
Rest.
1 × 100 yards individual medley.

STRETCH-OUT:

Medley of kicks Waterworks.
Bent knee marching step position.
Review dolphin circle.

Postpartum Workouts—Week 9

SWIM POINTERS:

· Shallow sitting dive.
· Interval swims.
· Ballet leg submarine.

REMINDERS:

Review shallow-water push-off.
Be certain water depth is sufficient (at least 4 feet) for shallow sitting dive practice.

WARM-UP:

Review breaststroke push-off.
Leg lifts and leg stretch Waterworks.
Ballet leg submarine (begin in bent knee position).
3 sitting dives. (Exit with push-up; use ladder only if needed.)

MAIN SWIM:

Level 1
  1 × 150 yards stroke choice.
  Rest.
  3 × 50 yards crawl on 2:00.

Level 2
  3 × 50 yards crawl on 1:30.
  1 × 200 yards stroke choice.
  Rest.
  3 × 50 yards crawl on 1:30.

Level 3
  1 × 100 yards individual medley.
  Rest.
  4 × 50 yards crawl on 1 minute.
  Rest.
  1 × 200 yards stroke choice.

Rest.
4 × 50 yards crawl on 1 minute.

STRETCH-OUT:

Review log roll and shark circle.
Ballet leg submarine.
3 sitting dives.

Postpartum Workouts—Week 10

SWIM POINTERS:

• Crouch position dive.
• Flamingo ballet leg submarine.
• Sidestroke medley.

REMINDERS:

For crouch position dive, be certain you're in deep enough water (approximately 5 feet).
Remember to push with your legs and bring them together in the air.

WARM-UP:

Pendulum body swing Waterworks.
Stationary sculling.
Clam.
Medley of kicks Waterworks.
3 crouch position dives.

MAIN SWIM:

Level 1
    1 × 100 yards sidestroke medley with variations on both sides:
        1 × 25 yards regular arm and regular scissors kick
        1 × 25 yards regular arm motion and inverted kick
        1 × 25 yards overarm variation and regular kick
        1 × 25 yards overarm variation and inverted kick.
    Rest.
    3 × 50 yards crawl stroke on 1:45.
    Rest.
    1 × 100 yards easy swim.

Level 2
    1 × 100 yards sidestroke medley with variations on both sides.
    Rest.
    3 × 50 yards crawl stroke on 1:30.

Rest.
1 × 200 yards stroke choice.
Rest.
2 × 50 yards crawl stroke on 1:20.

Level 3
1 × 100 yards sidestroke medley with variations on both sides.
5 × 50 yards crawl stroke on 1 minute.
1 × 300 yards stroke choice.
2 × 50 yards on 50 seconds.

STRETCH-OUT:

Hang ten Waterworks.
Treading.
Flamingo ballet leg submarine.
Crouch position dive.

Postpartum Workouts—Week 11

SWIM POINTERS:

- Standing dive.
- Vertical sculling position.
- Continuous swim.

REMINDERS:

Review crouch and semi-standing dives.

Place your back against the wall to help you practice proper body alignment for the vertical position.

WARM-UP:

Modified sit-ups Waterworks.
Scull foot first in vertical position.

MAIN SWIM:

Level 1

5-minute continuous swim, varying your strokes.
Rest.
3 × 50 yards on 1:45.

Level 2

8-minute continuous swim, varying your strokes.
Rest.
3 × 50 yards on 1:20.

Level 3

12-minute continuous swim, varying your strokes.
Rest.
5 × 50 yards on 1 minute.

STRETCH-OUT:

Medley of kicks Waterworks.
Medley of pulls Waterworks.
Head-first vertical position (handstand in 4-foot-deep water).

Postpartum Workouts—Week 12

SWIM POINTERS:

- Combinations of synchronized swimming figures and stroke variations to form a pattern (see chapter 23).
- 1 × 50 yards timed swim.

REMINDERS:

Smooth, graceful movements are basic to swimming and for synchronized swimming.
Vary strokes for continuous swim.

WARM-UP:

1 × 50 yards easy swim.
Synchronized swimming stroke variations and skills.

MAIN SWIM:

Level 1

5-minute continuous swim.
Rest.
2 × 25 yards synchronized swimming pattern: combine 2 figures with 2 stroke variations. Repeat sequence for entire lap. Rest between lengths.
1 × 50 yards crawl stroke, timed swim.

Level 2

8-minute continuous swim.
Rest.
2 × 25 yards synchronized swimming pattern: combine 3 figures with 3 stroke variations. Repeat sequence for entire lap.
Rest.
1 × 50 yards crawl stroke, timed swim.

Level 3

12-minute continuous swim.
Rest.
1 × 50 yards synchronized swimming pattern: combine 3 or more

figures with 3 or more stroke variations. Repeat sequence for entire lap.
Rest.
1 × 50 yards crawl stroke, timed swim.

STRETCH-OUT:

Review diving skills.
Medley of kicks Waterworks.
Medley of pulls Waterworks.
3 standing dives.

23

Introduction to Synchronized Swimming (Water Ballet)

Water ballet, known as the sport of synchronized swimming, consists of rhythmically performed swimming skills synchronized to music. In Europe, where it had its beginnings, it was also known as "ornamental swimming." The artistic nature of this aquatic activity is often compared to figure skating, as it combines the benefits of an art form with those of a sports activity. Synchronized swimming is now an Olympic sport and has come a long way since Esther Williams' time.

After your pregnancy, you can enjoy the benefits of this creative and graceful activity. You'll be using skills from your Waterworks exercises to learn synchronized swimming figures. These figures will be combined with your swim strokes to create beautiful movements and sequences in the water. You will find that toning and tightening your muscles, especially the abdominals, can be a beautiful as well as a beneficial experience.

Let there be music! Experiment with different types, tempos, and moods to create your own set of movements in a water routine. This graceful activity can be in addition to or an extension of your swimming workouts during and after your pregnancy. You can also adjust your movements to piped in music, or think of your favorite tune.

SWIMMING STROKE VARIATIONS FOR SYNCHRONIZED SWIMMING

Stroke	Head	Arm Motion	Leg Movement
Crawl	Head remains forward and out of water	Straight arm recovery	Bent knee flutter kick underwater
Breaststroke	Head remains out of water. Turn your head at the catch after each stroke	Hands splash on extension	Flutter kick underwater
Backstroke	Chin up Head remains still	Windmill backstroke or salute stroke	Slow bent knee flutter kick underwater
Sidestroke	Head remains still and/or alternates moving forward and back	Alternate overarm with regular arm pull	Alternate scissors with flutter kicks on glide

You can combine these swim stroke variations in the following ways:

- Alternate the crawl and backcrawl every three strokes.
- Alternate the sidestroke with the breaststroke, changing sides.
- Combine all the strokes while moving in the same direction—one breaststroke, one sidestroke, one backstroke, one crawl stroke, one breaststroke.
- Create your own combinations.

A basic component for executing and performing many of these synchronized swimming movements is sculling! It has been described as an arm motion for the backstroke, and in the "Waterworks" section it is described under treading. Sculling can be used in a variety of ways. It allows you to move in different directions and it supports your body in different positions.

There are several body positions that synchronized swimming utilizes. A sequence of movements within these positions is called a figure:

1. *Layout Position*

The body is in a horizontal position either on your back or your front. Your face, hips, thighs, and feet are close to the water's surface. Scull for support.

INTRODUCTION TO SYNCHRONIZED SWIMMING   191

EXAMPLES OF FIGURES IN LAYOUT POSITION

NAME: *Log Roll*

BENEFITS: Total body stretch.

STARTING POSITION: Begin in the supine or prone position, with one or both arms extended overhead.

HOW TO DO IT: Roll your body in either right or left direction by dropping your shoulder in the direction you wish to turn.

EXTRA TIPS: Try adding a flutter kick to move forward as you turn. The extra bulges you may get from pregnancy can be toned away nicely with the muscles used to maintain these positions.

NAME: *Marlin Turn*

BENEFITS: Total body stretch. Tones the entire body.

STARTING POSITION: Begin in a back layout position with your arms extended at shoulder level.

Marlin turn (¼ turn).

HOW TO DO IT: Your body will make four quarter (90°) turns on the surface of the water. To turn right, roll your body to the right one full turn as your legs move a quarter turn on the surface. Extend your arms out to your sides. Use them to move the legs and body to face a new direction. Roll your body to the left to turn left.

EXTRA TIPS: Your face may be above or below the surface as you complete each turn. Think of doing a log roll and add a quarter turn.

2. Tuck Position

The body is brought together in a compact position with the lower back rounded, knees together toward chest, and chin pressed to chest.

EXAMPLES OF FIGURES IN THE TUCK POSITION

NAME: *Tuck Turn*
BENEFITS: Tones entire body, especially the abdomen during postpartum. All your muscles can get a boost from this exercise if you use muscle power—do it with determination and purpose. This position may be beneficial in relieving lower back pain.

Tuck position (back).

STARTING POSITION: Begin in the back layout position.
HOW TO DO IT: Bring your knees toward your chest, keeping shins close to the water's surface. Remaining in the tuck position, turn your body 360°, pushing the water by turning your palms sideways in the opposite direction, keeping your face above the water. Repeat, going the other way.
EXTRA TIPS: If you drop your hips, your feet should not pop up—this is similar to the Waterworks sit-up position.

3. Pike Position

Your body is at approximately a 90° angle at the hips—your straightened legs are drawn toward your chest. This can be done in the supine or prone position.

EXAMPLES OF FIGURES IN THE PIKE POSITION

NAME: *Clam*
BENEFITS: For toning abdomen and stretching lower leg muscles.
STARTING POSITION: Begin in a back layout position.

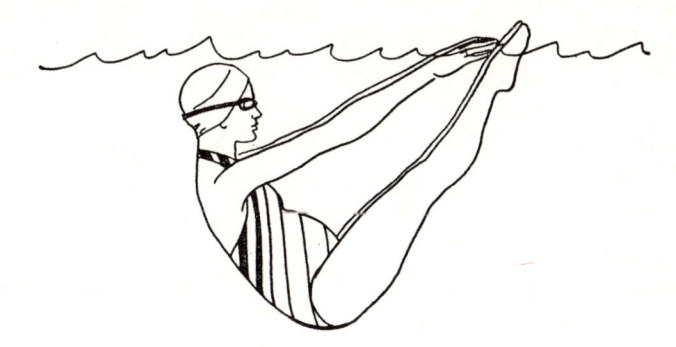

Pike position.

HOW TO DO IT: With your arms, create a downward and overhead circular movement as the hips pike. Your hands then move out of the water to approach your feet before submerging.

EXTRA TIPS: As your abdomen increases in strength, pike your hips more, trying to touch your hands to your feet. Remember to stretch and point your toes.

4. Ballet Leg Position

Your body is in an extended back layout position with your toes pointed. Sculling close to your hips is used to maintain your position. One leg bends at the knee toward your chest and then extends to the ceiling. The other leg remains on the surface of the water. Ideally, your legs will form a 90° angle. There are many exercise figures and hybrids that begin in this position. A few examples follow—create your own, too.

EXAMPLES OF FIGURES IN THE BALLET LEG POSITION

NAME: *The Bent-Knee Marching Step Position*
BENEFITS: Total body exercise for toning arms and abdomen, especially good during the postpartum shape-up. Toning helps the arms, which helps the chest, which helps the waist, etc.—wonderful!
STARTING POSITION: Begin in the back layout position.
HOW TO DO IT: Lift and bend one leg so that your thigh is perpendicular to the water's surface.

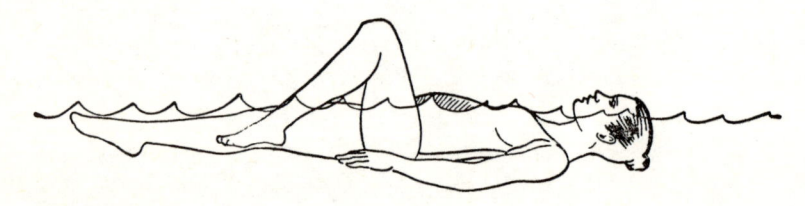

Bent knee position.

EXTRA TIPS: Try moving in a headfirst direction by flexing your wrists and pointing your fingers up slightly as you scull.
Try alternately bending both legs.
If you are having difficulty keeping the straight leg on the surface, place it on the pool's edge or have someone support you lightly under your ankle.

NAME: *Ballet Leg Submarine and Variations*
BENEFITS: Total body exercise.
STARTING POSITION: Assume the ballet leg position.
HOW TO DO IT: Maintaining the ballet leg position, let your body drop below the water's surface by turning your palms upward, then return to the surface by sculling vigorously. Try to keep your knees straight.
EXTRA TIPS: Alternate ballet legs.
You may also practice this exercise using a kickboard and the edge of the pool, as illustrated.

Practice ballet leg position at edge of pool, using kickboard to support arm.

Double ballet leg position.

OTHER VARIATIONS: Double ballet legs—begin from the tuck position. Extend your legs so that they are both perpendicular to the water's surface. You can do a submarine in this position as well, lowering your body so that the water line is at ankle level.

For variety, try the flamingo ballet leg submarine. Begin in the tuck position and extend one leg to the ballet leg position. Change leg positions and submerge in this position.

5. Circle Position (Arched)

The body is arched so that your head, buttocks, and feet follow the arc of the circumference of a circle. *This position should only be done during the early stages of your pregnancy and during the postpartum period.*

EXAMPLES OF FIGURES IN THE CIRCLE POSITION

NAME: *Shark Circle*
BENEFITS: This exercise stretches your sides and abdomen. Sometimes holding the new baby will put special strain on this part of your body—tone it up now and avoid problems later.

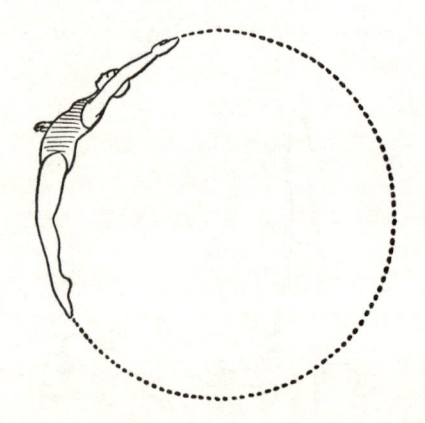

Shark circle position.

STARTING POSITION: Begin in a back layout floating position. Turn to either side to assume a side layout position with the top arm extended overhead. The arm should be next to your ear, close to the water's surface.
HOW TO DO IT: Scull with your lower arm to move your body in a complete circle on the surface. Complete your shark circle by resuming your back layout position.
EXTRA TIPS: If you need an extra boost for propulsion, add a small flutter kick. Keep your back arched evenly throughout your circle.

NAME: *Dolphin Circle*
BENEFITS: This figure helps your entire body move underwater and works against the water's buoyancy. It stretches lower back and side areas and helps you practice holding your breath.

STARTING POSITION: Begin in deep water in the back layout position.

HOW TO DO IT: With your head leading, move the body backward in an underwater circle (6–7 foot diameter). Begin sculling with your arms overhead to initiate the circle; then, as you continue the circle, scull at your hips until you finish in the back layout position.

EXTRA TIPS: Begin to practice the dolphin circle by first pushing off from the wall—use the backstroke start.

Use a pair of nose clips, exhale continuously through both your nose and mouth to keep water out.

For variation, bend one knee as you circle or try doing the dolphin circle going foot first by placing your hands under your hips, fingers pointed downward.

6. Vertical Position

The body is positioned with the hips, head, and ankles in line and at right angles to the water's surface. These positions will help you to return to your proper body alignment during your postpartum period.

EXAMPLES OF FIGURES IN THE VERTICAL POSITION

NAME: *Foot-First Vertical (with underwater support sculling)*

BENEFITS: Helps your posture and helps to increase your breath control.

STARTING POSITION: Place your back against the wall in water just over your head (about 6 feet). All your body parts should be aligned: head, back, hips, legs, etc. Press your elbows to your sides at the waist bending your elbows at 90°.

HOW TO DO IT: Keep your palms facing up and elbows at your sides, move your forearms outward toward your sides, and then return them to the front of your body. Continue this movement vigorously with no hesitations. Try to lower with your "support scull" so that your toes touch bottom.

EXTRA TIPS: Try to keep your head, back, buttocks, and heels close to the wall as you lower. Exhaling will allow you to sink easily.

NAME: *Head-First Vertical*

BENEFITS: Teaches you to balance your body in a handstand vertical position.

STARTING POSITION: Begin by standing in chest-deep water.

HOW TO DO IT: Begin by standing and then lean forward and assume the tuck position with feet off the bottom. Place your hands on the pool floor. Slowly lift your legs overhead to a vertical handstand. Return to the standing position.

EXTRA TIPS: Keep chin on chest. Move slowly so that you can maintain balance with your fingertips.

VERTICAL VARIATIONS: Try these from either a front pike position or from a vertical.

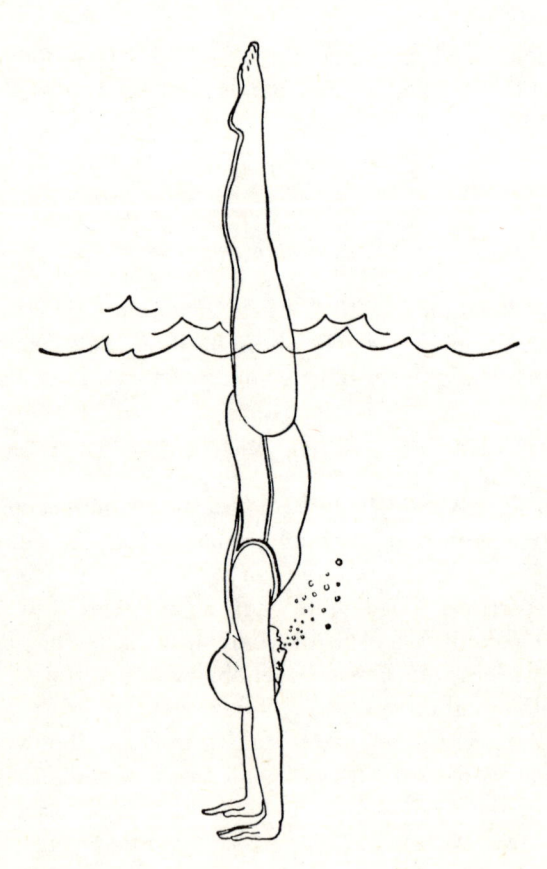

Head-first vertical position.

"V" LEG SPLIT POSITION: Open legs evenly forward and back or to the side from your handstand position.

The figures described above are usually done solo; however, they can be done as duets. Below are some examples of duet or paired figures.

Duet Figures

An important facet of these figures is contact with your swimming partner, both for aesthetic effect and for physical support. Have your coach join you!

NAME: *Plank*

BENEFITS: This is fun to do as well as giving you and your partner a total body stretch; too, an often overlooked aspect of the postpartum period is contact touching, and the plank provides that.

STARTING POSITION: Begin with both partners in back layout position with one partner grasping the ankles of the other forming a "plank" with their bodies.

HOW TO DO IT: The partner who holds the other's ankles submerges slightly as she maintains her back layout position. She then pulls the other over her head in order to exchange positions. Now you're ready for another plank exchange.

EXTRA TIPS: Maintain a streamlined position when pulling. Exchange places several times.

NAME: *Water Wheel*

BENEFITS: This is a stretch and it looks great too! It can be done before and after your baby's birth—have your coach try this with you.

STARTING POSITION: Begin in the back layout position alone by bending one knee out to the side and placing your foot next to the knee of the straight leg. Partner assumes the same water wheel position, placing her head next to the foot of your extended leg.

HOW TO DO IT: Grasp each other's ankle with your near arm; then each of you scull with your outside arm to turn your bodies on the surface in the direction of your bent knee.

EXTRA TIPS: To get the feel of the water wheel position, have your partner stand beside your extended leg to help support you.

Change outside leg's position as you rotate.

Extend legs in a V position.

Team or Group Swimming

Group figures can be done with three or more people. (Usually a group or team routine is done with four to eight people.) Group figures are fun and include the following:

Star formation
Circle float pattern
Chain log roll and chain dolphin. To maintain a chain, point your toes and hold your partner's head gently with your feet around his neck.

A routine could include combinations of all of these.

Tandem Strokes/Sculling

Tandem sculling: Scull hooked together in various combinations: either feet to feet or head to toes, hand to hand, back to back, etc. Vary and create your own combinations.

Synchronized Swimming Workout

This workout has many valuable components; however, you are encouraged to pick and choose whatever parts you wish to try.

WARM-UP:

- Slow deepwater bobbing.
- 50 yards of easy crawl.
- 50 yards of windmill backstroke.
- Easy treading in place. Try lifting your arms out of the water and supporting yourself with your legs only.

MAIN SWIM:

(Do more or less depending on your skill and stamina.)
- Scull 25 yards, head first (fingers upward), back layout position.
- Scull 25 yards, feet first (fingers downward), back layout position.
- Tuck turns:
    at the wall
    to the right
    to the left
- Swim the width of the pool *underwater* using the breaststroke. (Swim as far as you comfortably can underwater if you cannot make it across 1 width.)
- Return using an easy breaststroke.

STROKE SKILLS: (Use synchronized stroke variations)

- Swim 25 yards using the crawl stroke and the backstroke.
- Swim 25 yards using the breaststroke and the sidestroke.
- Swim 50 yards creating your own stroke variations.

FIGURE AND STROKE COMBINATIONS:

- Repeat the following sequence for 25 yards: 3 crawl strokes with head up, log roll, 3 backstrokes, and clam, until you reach the wall.
- At the wall, turn with a half shark circle.
- Repeat the following sequence for 25 yards: 2 sidestrokes, 2 breaststrokes, front pike somersault.
- *Ballet Legs:* In the supine position with your toes on the lip of the pool, scull as you bend your knees (marching steps); then lift one leg to the extended ballet leg position.
- *Support Sculling:* With your back against the wall, lower your body underwater as far as possible while sculling. Repeat.

STRETCH-OUT:

- Slowly complete 4 marlin turns (4 quarter turns in place).
- Easy sculling for 25 yards.
- Swim using the inverted breaststroke for 25 yards (enjoy the full glide).
- Swim gently for 50 yards.
- Leg and arm stretches at the wall.

24

Introductory Diving Progression

Perhaps you haven't had an opportunity to dive or to learn how to enter the water head first. Now is as good a time as any to learn. *Important:* Do not dive during pregnancy!

General Diving Tips for Head-First Entries

- Remove your goggles.
- Keep your chin on your chest.
- Angle your arms at 45° to the water's surface and hook your thumbs together.
- Straighten your legs as you push.
- Keep your body streamlined in the glide position for the recovery.

Shallow Sitting Dive

Safety Check: You should only attempt this dive at a pool depth of 4 feet or deeper.

First of all, review your push-off into a prone glide.

Begin by sitting on the top step of the ladder or stairs, or on the pool deck. Place the balls of your feet on the very edge and curl your toes for an extra grip.

INTRODUCTORY DIVING PROGRESSION

Extend your arms over your ears, keep your chin down on your chest, and point your hands downward at a 45° angle to the water's surface. Push with your legs as your body straightens and streamlines for entry, and glide into the water with your fingers pointing first.

Crouch Position Dive

This is the next step for a head-first entry. Remember the elements are the same as in the shallow sitting dive. Always protect your head by keeping your arms in front.

To begin, stand on the deck with one foot forward and curled over the edge. Slowly bend your knees to a comfortable level and bend at the waist. Place your hands over your ears at a 45° downward angle to the water's edge. Keep your chin on your chest, lean forward, push with both legs, and bring them together before they submerge.

Semi-Standing Dive

This is a transition dive before the full standing dive, and it emphasizes a reduction in the bend of the knees in the crouch position.

Standing Dive

To begin, stand on the deck with both feet curled over the edge. Bend or pike at the waist with your arms extended at a 45° angle to the water's surface, looking at your knees. Fall forward, keeping this position; push off slightly and then straighten your legs to give a little height to your dive. Gradually decrease the angle of your arms to the water.

Recommended depth for this dive is 6 feet.

25

Introductory Butterfly Skills

Perhaps you're saying to yourself, right now, "Let's skip this stroke...." But wait: the exciting, graceful butterfly stroke is not beyond your abilities.

The arm motion for the butterfly is actually the S-pull crawl motion, done using both arms simultaneously with an overwater recovery.

The butterfly leg motion is called the dolphin kick, and it is similar to the flutter kick, except that the legs move simultaneously. You can also use the frog kick.

Your breathing pattern is similar to that used with the breaststroke.

A wavelike body motion is done continuously when swimming the butterfly. It resembles the diving motion of a dolphin.

There is no denying that the butterfly is a strenuous stroke, but it can be done in the following progression.

Butterfly Arm Motion

- Standing in waist-deep water, make big forward circles, moving both arms together and recovering out of the water with your elbows slightly bent.
- Walk forward as you pull.
- Bend forward slightly from the waist to add the S-pull to your arm motion.
- Remember to move your arms simultaneously and make an hourglass or

INTRODUCTORY BUTTERFLY SKILLS   205

question mark shape with them. Keep your elbows higher than your hands as in the crawl stroke.

Butterfly Leg Motion (Dolphin Kick)

- Sit on the deck of the pool, keeping your feet together. Bend your knees so that you touch your heels against the wall under the water, then straighten your legs, pushing the water with your shins.
- As a variation, float in a prone position holding on to the wall, and kick by using a small up-and-down wavelike motion.
- Try the butterfly dolphin kick either unassisted or with a kickboard, and with or without fins. Your heels should just break the water's surface.
- When you're ready, try a two-beat kick by pausing slightly after every two kicks.

Coordination and Breathing

- Coordinate one arm cycle with one kick (either dolphin or frog).
- Try the two-beat dolphin kick. First kick as your arms enter the water (the catch); the second kick is done as your arms finish pulling and are ready to recover.
- Breathing: Inhale on the pull and exhale as you recover.
    – Inhale whenever needed.
    – Inhale every stroke cycle.
    – Try alternate breathing by inhaling at every other stroke cycle.

Butterfly Stroke Variation: Double Arm Backstroke

- The double arm backstroke is a combination of several of the strokes already described.

    Arms. Pull and recover your arms as in the windmill backstroke, but move your arms simultaneously and glide with your arms at your sides.
    Legs. Use either the whip kick or the flutter kick.
    Coordination. On the glide, your arms will be at your sides and your legs will be together. As you kick, your arms will recover out of the water.
- Try "flutterfly" (a combination of the butterfly and crawl stroke or breaststroke components):
    – crawl arm motion with dolphin kick

- butterfly pull with flutter kick
- butterfly arm motion with frog kick.
- Butterfly arm motion with dolphin kick (single kick then the two-beat kick).

Although the above sounds quite strenuous, give it a try. Begin with short distances and work up to a maximum distance of 25 yards at any one time.

V
Family Swim Tips

Introduction

Swimming is the ideal family activity—fun and safe for all.

One of the best gifts you can give your child is to teach him or her how to safely enjoy the pleasures of swimming and water play. It's a gift your child will keep for life. And with the right approach, it's a gift you will enjoy giving as much as your child will enjoy receiving.

You can introduce your child to the joys of water almost immediately after birth. Remember, a water environment is familiar to your infant, as he has just spent nine months in amniotic fluid. An infant in water will instinctively paddle and hold his breath if he submerges (although he will lack the strength to get his face above the water to breathe).

It is very important to project the right attitude when introducing your baby to water. Your baby will enjoy the water only if he senses that you are comfortable and confident in and about the water. Babies are very receptive to the emotions of people around them, and if your infant senses that you are afraid or uncomfortable, then he will tend to find his experience in the water unpleasant and even frightening. Children learn to be afraid of the water; it is not an innate response.

The benefits of teaching your infant to enjoy and maneuver in water are clear. If you bring your infant to the water, using the proper approach, you'll be starting him on the road to a lifetime of safety, fun, and fitness. You will aid in the development of your baby's muscular strength, coordination, and balance. There are even some indications that children who engage in water play and swimming at an early age are healthier, more intelligent, and more sociable than those who don't—a real plus for your child. And of course teaching your baby how to stay afloat will give him an important safety skill. In addition, you will find that as you work with your baby in the water, there is a wonderful and very special bonding that develops that can enhance your relationship forever.

Of course, you must use common sense in working with your baby in the water. You have to remember that your baby has no control over his world, and you should be careful to avoid shocks of temperature changes, sudden immersions, or rough water. You should also take care and keep a close watch on your baby's health and the hygiene of the swimming facility. *Never, ever, leave your baby alone in or around water,* or divert your attention from your baby even for a moment. Keep your expectations reasonable—no two-year-old is ready to swim the length of a pool. You may have seen television or magazine reports of the seemingly astounding capabilities of so-called "water babies," but be aware that movies of babies swimming for long periods usually are staged and edited, and that few if any infants can swim alone for more than several seconds. A child usually is physically capable of sustained independent swimming only when he reaches the age of three.

If you use common sense and care, you and your baby will both have a truly wonderful, rewarding experience in the water. And you may find that you will learn things about your baby and your relationship with him or her.

27

Water Play with Your Newborn—
Do Go Near the Water!

It's never too early to start teaching your infant to love the water. The best way to start is to try to make your newborn's baths as pleasant as possible for him. Remember, your baby will be sensitive to your feelings, so make sure that you bring a positive attitude.

Your newborn will be ready for his first bath about two weeks after his birth. Time his first bath so that it takes place when he is in a happy mood, and do it where he will be most comfortable. Don't start the bath when he is hungry or tired or crying for any reason.

Never, ever, under any circumstances divert your attention from your infant for a second when he is in the bath. Let the telephone or door go unanswered while you bathe your baby. Better yet, take the telephone receiver off the hook.

Make sure the water in your baby's tub or sink is comfortable—about body temperature. If you're uncertain, check the temperature with a thermometer, since a temperature that feels comfortable to you may be extremely unpleasant to your baby.

The sink or basin should be about one half filled with water.

Your newborn's first immersion in water should be a comfortable, secure experience. When you place your baby in the sink or tub, support his head and neck with one hand, and gently lower him into the water while maintaining eye contact, smiling, and speaking soothingly to him. Submerge your baby slowly feet first; only half to two thirds of your baby's body should be below the water's surface. Your baby should be on his back in a semi-upright position. He should never be left lying flat. Always elevate his head higher than his hips.

Try to make your baby's bath fun. Play with the baby and provide appropriate water toys.

When you play with your baby in the water, try to include love pats and tickling, as well as gentle rocking. You may also wish to stretch your baby's arms across his chest, to the sides, and overhead. Bend and flex baby's hands and feet and move his legs in a bicycling motion; these motions will help your newborn develop motor control and strength.

Save water and bathe with your baby. When he's a few weeks old, let your baby join you in the tub. Lie back in the tub and place the baby on your abdomen. Enjoy relaxing in the water and your baby's closeness.

28

Infants

As your baby grows, you will be able to teach him new water skills. Between six months and approximately a year and a half, he can learn some basic water safety skills and exercises. Rarely will a child younger than two years old be able to master conventional swimming techniques. But even at this infant stage he'll be capable of learning to maneuver more in the water.

Always make sure that the pool is clean, the air is warm, and the water temperature is comfortable, and there is a secure part of the pool where you and your baby will not be bothered by other swimmers or exposed to pool turbulence. Always stay in standing depth only. Keep your baby in the water for a maximum of half an hour at a time, and try to get into the pool one to three times per week. Make sure your pediatrician is aware of your baby's pool activities.

What can you expect to teach your baby before he walks? Some courses on infant swimming claim that babies of this age can be taught to kick, breathe, float, and turn over in the water and paddle a few feet to the edge of the pool for safety. You may consider enrolling you and your baby in such a course. However, whether you've joined a class or you're taking your little one swimming on your own, it's most important to instill in your baby a love for the water and a sense of security as you teach him some basic water skills. His lessons will also help strengthen his muscles, develop his balance and coordination, and perhaps teach him how to relax, play, and maneuver in the water. It's vital to have a positive outlook about your pool experience.

Spending time with your baby in the water is special and unique and can add to your relationship. Where else are you with your child free from intrusions and distractions such as telephone calls and unexpected visitors? To make sure that your child benefits as much as possible from this water experience, you should create a happy, pleasant, secure environment. Remember to maintain eye contact with your baby while you're both in the water; smile, talk to your child, cuddle, kiss, pat, and even try singing! If you feel good and confident in the water, your baby will respond to your enthusiasm.

Try the following exercises to teach your baby basic water skills.

Start by simply cuddling your baby in the water, with his body submerged so that he can get the feel of the water. Walk across the width of the pool. Pay close attention to him at all times, being careful to support his face out of the water. Since baby's head is proportionately heavier at this stage of growth, remember to keep his hips lower than his shoulders.

Introducing baby to the water.

Your baby will quickly learn to enjoy this new environment. Use your hands to gently wet his face with the water so that he becomes comfortable with the feeling of water gently coming over his head. Your baby may be startled at first, so be sure to reassure him as you do this.

Next try bobbing with your baby just as you do to warm up. This is a lot of fun for the baby. Hold him upright, gently lifting and lowering him in the water so that he submerges to shoulder level. As he learns to enjoy this, increase the range of motion until he submerges to the neck.

Next, combine bobbing with breath control. In a face to face position, lower the baby's mouth and yours to the surface of the water. If the baby responds positively, then try to lower him to cover more of his face in the water. Eventually lower him and yourself to eyebrow level. Make sure that he is under water only for a moment. Smile, compliment, kiss, and soothe him when he emerges. Eventually your baby will learn to hold his breath for a few seconds and enjoy the feeling of submerging.

Hold your baby around his chest, thumbs at nipple level, facing you. Be careful to hold him high enough so that his face is out of the water, keeping his head higher than his hips. Slowly walk backward so that your baby is drawn through the water. Don't forget the positive reinforcements—smiling, cuddling, and talking.

You can give your baby a feeling of floating by holding and swirling him on his back, being sure that his face is out of the water. You should support baby's head and neck with both hands as you walk backward and maintain eye contact. Baby's legs may begin a crawling, kicking motion.

Later you can try swirling him on his back by holding his hands and extending his arms overhead.

You can teach your infant how to paddle in the water by imitating a crawling movement. With one hand, hold him in the water in a prone position, making sure his face is out of the water. With your free hand, move his legs in a crawling motion until he gets the idea and continues to "kick" by himself. Move your baby forward as you walk backward through the water as he kicks. When he is familiar with kicking, hold him at the waist with one hand and use your free hand to start his arms moving in a crawling motion until he tries the movement on his own. When he is able to do both arm and leg movements, try releasing him momentarily. Be ready to support him if he starts to submerge or tire. You must be patient; it may take some weeks or months of training practice before your baby can use these skills effectively.

Try this when possible: two adults standing several feet apart can pass the baby to one another. The baby will be momentarily free of support in the water, as the baby is gently pushed toward open arms and a smiling face.

When your baby has developed a grasp, he will be able to learn to hang on to the edge of the pool and hold his head up. This is an important safety skill. Hold your baby at the pool wall with his head up and his body in the water. Place his hands on the edge, holding his hands there as you support his body. Gradually transfer your support from his body to his arms so that he is supported by his arms as he grasps the pool edge. Be sure to smile and talk to him as he does this. Repeat this, gradually giving your baby less support on his arms, until he can hold on by himself. Additional skills your baby can learn are a safe entry and exit to and from the pool deck. Baby can enter from the edge of the pool by falling forward into your arms. Position baby back to the edge of pool after entry. Eventually baby will learn to paddle to the pool edge.

29

Toddler Stage—The Terrible Two's

During his toddler stage, approximately one and a half to three years of age, your baby will go through one of the most important phases of his education. A child is extraordinarily receptive during this period of his life, very curious and adventurous. In fact, some experts contend that a child will experience approximately 60 percent of the development of his personality and attitudes during his toddler stage. Take advantage of this to impart to your baby a love of the water and to teach him basic water skills.

One of the best ways to teach your child during his toddler stage is repetition. Although you should include a variety of games and exercises in your water play with your child, it is very important to repeat games and exercises so that your child develops familiarity and facility with the water skills involved in the games. You'll probably find that your baby enjoys playing games he is familiar with rather than continually being exposed to new games.

As your baby grows, he will be capable of acquiring new water skills and techniques. Practicing these skills and techniques will aid in his physical and emotional development.

In the toddler stage your child most likely will be able to learn to move through the water, prone and supine, perhaps with a push; to bob in the water to a limited extent, breathing when he emerges; to enter the water by jumping in and surfacing; and perhaps a simple stroking motion, based on the movements used in crawling, which can support him and permit him to maneuver in the water for a limited period of time. In fact, some classes for toddlers even teach them to swim through underwater hoops.

Teaching toddlers to "swim" through underwater hoops.

Now is the time to teach your toddler to blow bubbles underwater. Begin by teaching him to blow bubbles on the surface of the water. Make analogies to blowing through a straw or blowing out birthday candles. Next do the "submarine." Walk backward while holding toddler face to face, giving him the feeling of movement. At the count of 3, gently lower for a moment underwater. Be sure to kiss, praise, and cuddle after each submarine.

You can also improvise a "magic slide." Place a kickboard or inflatable plastic raft over the edge of the pool. Gently place baby tummy down on the slide so that he enters head first, wide-eyed, and into open arms

TODDLER STAGE—THE TERRIBLE TWO'S

and a kiss from his parent. When he is more advanced he can "swim" to and reach for colorful objects under the water.

It's very important to make your baby's swim time as much fun as possible during his toddler stage. Supply him with water toys, such as balls and inflatable animals, for his water play. Combine the play with the development of skills, strength, and coordination. For instance, you can have your little one paddle a few feet to retrieve a toy, or you can teach him breath control by making a game of reaching underwater for colorful objects. Also try pushing him in a front float, upon a signal, to the pool's edge.

During your baby's toddler stage, you may consider obtaining a small outdoor wading pool for him to use. Of course, as always, you should never leave him unattended in the pool, and you should always empty the pool if you are not going to be available to watch it. (I recommend that you buy a pool that can easily be emptied by one adult. Remember that even a small pool will be very heavy when full of water.) Fill the pool only with several inches of water, and keep a supply of toys such as balls and other floating objects available.

30

Preschoolers

Between three and five years of age, your preschool child will be able to master some more of the basic swimming skills and to participate in a swimming program that will help him develop a fit and healthy body, as well as have a love of the water.

A child of preschool age is ready to be enrolled in an organized program where he can learn proper swimming techniques and water safety. Often the facilities used in these programs and classes have a raised platform placed in the pool that adjusts the pool depth to about two feet. Look for a preschool program run by experienced staff that places priority on water safety. Swimming programs for children three to five, if well designed, should be progressive in nature.

What swimming skills can you expect your child to learn at this age? Most children will be able to learn water adjustment skills, breathing techniques, prone and supine floats, a basic crawl stroke, and how to change positions in the water from back to front and vice versa.

Although you may not be directly involved in the water with your child's swimming program at this stage, encouragement from you will make a big difference in how well your child participates and enjoys the program. Make a point of swimming with your child outside of his regular program, keeping abreast of his accomplishments, helping him master skills, and encouraging him. He'll get a lot more out of his program, and so will you. Remember, it's a family affair!

Here are some brief descriptions of water activities you can do with your child:

Review skills already learned and those he may now be learning in his class. Use the "train and engineer" position to practice skills in prone position. This is done by having child face you and place his hands on your shoulders. You support him in the prone position by placing your hands under his hips. He can practice breathing techniques and flutter kicking. You walk backward (engineer) as your child kicks and locomotes forward (train).

Your child can also practice these skills if you place one kickboard under each of his arms for support. His arms should be resting on the boards at the surface, with elbows bent, so that the kickboards are not below the surface of the water. You must stand in front of your child and guide him by lightly holding on to the front end of the boards.

Another activity is tossing pennies to the pool bottom for him to find and retrieve. Your child learns to open his eyes and hold his breath.

Another favorite game is the "whale ride." Your child holds your shoulders piggyback style. You take him for a ride around the shallow area, and on the child's oral command "whale," you dip under the water for a moment.

31

Youngsters—Age Six to Teens

At age six your child should be capable of learning all of the basic swimming skills and strokes. Now is the time to give your child more formal aquatic training. This training could prepare him for participation in a competitive swimming program. These programs are usually open to children between the ages of eight and eighteen years of age. Competitive programs will vary in what they require from their participants, how much instruction and coaching the child will receive, and how important competition is in the program. As a parent you should compare these factors with what you know about your child's maturity, adequacy of prior experiences, and his motivation to determine what is best for your speedster.

Competitive programs are available at community recreation and school facilities, and private swim clubs.

VI

Common Q's and Uncommon A's

32

Swimming During Your Pregnancy

Q. Why should I swim during my pregnancy?
A. There are at least three reasons for swimming during your pregnancy. First, a proper swimming and water exercise program will help to prepare you for the physical and emotional demands of labor and will make your delivery easier. Second, a proper program will make your pregnancy more comfortable and enjoyable. Third, swimming will improve your aerobic fitness, strength, and flexibility while avoiding overexertion, stress, and shock.

Q. Is this swimming program appropriate for pregnant women of all ages?
A. The program is suitable for all mothers-to-be, provided they have obtained their doctors' approval.

Q. What do women who have swum through their pregnancies say?
A. Here are some samples of what they had to say:

- "I swam two to three times per week and felt great!"
- "Move slower, give yourself more time to get in and out of the pool. Look forward to introducing the baby to the joys and wonder of water."
- "I stopped jogging because I felt like something was coming loose, but I had no fear of swimming during pregnancy. . . . I loved the

tranquil feeling and had no fear that I would injure the baby. Swimming works your body out in a nonviolent way."
- "I swam half a mile three times per week until two weeks prior to delivery."
- "Swimming kept my weight down."
- "I liked the warm water."
- "I could tell the difference in how I felt, physically, if I swam and didn't swim."
- "I felt tight if I didn't swim."
- "Three times per week was average. I didn't want to exhaust myself."

Q. Can I use a Jacuzzi or a hot tub during my pregnancy?
A. No. Instead, if you wish, sit in the pool next to a water jet.

Q. Do women who swam through their pregnancies feel it was beneficial?
A. Women report that swimming really helped make their pregnancies more enjoyable. They felt better about their bodies and in the best possible physical condition for labor and delivery.

Q. Why do I feel the need to urinate often?
A. The capacity of the bladder is diminished because the uterus is sitting and pressing on the top of the bladder, causing you to urinate more often.

Q. What causes the discomfort in my lower back in my third trimester?
A. It could be that your baby has turned 180° in your womb, and you feel this in your lower back. To relieve the discomfort, you should get the weight of the baby off your spine. Lie on your side. Your partner (coach) should massage your lower back by pushing gently in at your lower back and pulling on your hip. This will help to shift the angle of your hip and help relieve the back pain. Try applying ice packs on your lower back and have your coach massage your lower back by rolling his fist along your back—these also help to relieve some of the pain.

Q. How do I know if my water has broken when I am swimming?
A. You actually may not know. However, if it breaks in the water, you may feel a gush of warm water as you're swimming. In that case, leave the pool immediately to avoid any possible infection.

Q. What is a useful gift idea for a parent-to-be?
A. Consider giving a membership in a health club, or a recreation center with a twenty-five-yard pool, or a wristwatch with a stop-watch function.

Q. Are there any organizations that I could contact for further information?
A. The Amateur Swimming Association have a working party currently looking into all aspects of prenatal swimming, and are planning a leaflet on this subject. They can also supply details of mother and baby swimming classes in your area. Write to them at:
The Amateur Swimming Association
Derby Street
Loughborough
Leicestershire LE11 0AL

33

About Health, Beauty, and Safety Q's

Q. If I swim during my pregnancy, do I need any special foods?
A. During your pregnancy, whether you swim or not, you don't have to drastically change your diet (although if you're unaccustomed to swimming, you may have to increase your food intake to supply the extra calories you will burn off while swimming). Consult your doctor. You may wish to increase your intake of fresh fruits, fluids, vegetables, and whole grains. You should avoid junk food, processed food, food additives, caffeine, salt, tobacco, and alcohol.

Q. Should I take a vitamin and/or mineral supplement during my pregnancy?
A. Check your diet and nutritional needs with your doctor. Some women may require vitamin and/or mineral supplements, especially iron supplements, during their pregnancy, but you should not take any substance without your doctor's approval.

Q. Do I have to eat for two?
A. No, not really, although your intake of food may increase somewhat during your pregnancy. Again, check with your doctor. Remember that if you gain more than thirty pounds during your pregnancy, you will probably be left with excess fat on your body after giving birth.

Q. Since I've been pregnant, I've felt that I've had a cold continuously. Should this stop me from swimming?

A. Because pregnancy-related hormonal changes affect the mucous membranes of some women, increasing mucous secretion, these women feel as if they have colds throughout their pregnancies. You may be one of these women. This condition should not prevent you from swimming during your pregnancy; in fact, swimming may help you feel better.

Q. Since I've been pregnant, I've developed varicose veins. How will swimming affect this condition?
A. Varicose veins during pregnancy result from the inability of the blood collected in lower extremities to return to the heart and upper body. This happens because pregnancy puts extra demands on the circulatory system, causing valves in the veins to weaken. A proper swimming and water exercise program will strengthen your circulatory system and may help to alleviate the condition. In addition, the buoyancy of the water can help to relieve demands on the circulatory system and so ease the discomfort of varicose veins.

Q. Can swimming cause a vaginal infection?
A. Actually, little water enters the vagina during swimming because of the overlap of the anterior and posterior walls. Also, the forward direction of the body through the water helps to prevent any water from forcefully entering the vaginal area. Of course, clean pool water will minimize the risk of infection. A clean pool is a safe pool, but a pool with "ring around the collar" is a pool you should bypass. If you do develop a mild vaginal infection, you do not necessarily have to stop swimming, but check with your doctor.

Q. If I swim during my pregnancy, can I suffer ill effects from the chlorine?
A. No. Proper use of chlorine will keep the pool free of bacteria and algae. The chlorine will not cause you or your unborn child any ill effects. Chlorine helps to keep the water clear. Use goggles to protect your eyes from possible chlorine irritation.

Q. Can you suggest some general safety tips for swimming during pregnancy?
A. You must keep your doctor apprised of your exercise program and conform to his advice. You should never push yourself too hard; be guided by how you feel; if you ever experience pain or bleeding, stop exercising and see your doctor. Follow these basic safety rules:

1. Never swim alone.
2. Never indulge in alcohol while swimming.
3. If you swim in a natural body of water, be aware of currents and tides.
4. Don't overestimate your abilities.
5. Don't swim immediately after eating a heavy meal.
6. Leave the water if you feel chilly or numb, or if your lips or fingers become blue.

Q. Should I do anything to protect my skin after swimming?
A. It is advisable to shower after a swim, to remove chlorinated water. Follow your shower with the application of a moisturizing lotion to replace natural skin oils that are removed by the pool water.

Q. What should I do for my hair?
A. To protect your hair while swimming, you may wish to wear a rubber bathing cap. (I recommend that you wear two caps, a stretch cap covered with a rubber cap.) Some swimmers apply a little baby oil or conditioner to their hair before swimming. Wash your hair after you swim, and apply a conditioner. You may wish to choose a hair style that is manageable with frequent washings.

Q. Should I stay out of the sun during my pregnancy?
A. You should stay out of the sun during your pregnancy because you are more susceptible to a condition called "chloasma" or "melasma" (sometimes called the "mask of pregnancy"). This is an excess of pigmentation brought about by exposure to the sun, which most often appears on the upper lip, cheeks, and forehead. Any woman can get this condition, but because of your elevated hormone level during your pregnancy, you are more susceptible.

If you are going into the sun for any reason, use a sunscreen with a sun protection factor (SPF) of 15.

34

Postpartum Period

Q. How soon after giving birth can I resume swimming?
A. Most women are ready to resume swimming within four to six weeks after giving birth, but you should have your doctor's approval before you start. Of course, in no event should you resume swimming until all pregnancy-related surgery has completely healed.

Q. Will it be difficult to resume swimming after giving birth?
A. You should not have any physical difficulty resuming swimming after you've recovered from giving birth. You may have problems motivating yourself, however. There are a million excuses (none of them good), such as "I won't look good in a bathing suit," or "I'm tired, and besides I'm too busy with the baby." To help overcome these, keep in mind that a good swimming program will not only make you healthier and fitter, it will give you extra energy for caring for and enjoying your baby. It will also help you recover and perhaps even improve your former figure.

Q. Can I swim when I'm menstruating?
A. If you use a tampon you can swim during menstruation with no problems or ill effects. Competitive swimmers do not stop swimming when they have their periods, and neither should you.

Q. Is there a higher risk of vaginal infections if I swim during my period?

A. No. The vagina will not admit water unless that water is forced in under pressure, and there has been no evidence to support the idea that you run a higher risk of vaginal infection while swimming during your period.

Q. Will exercise affect my ability to breast-feed my baby?
A. No. Exercising, especially swimming, will improve your circulation, which will help your milk production.

Q. What is sports gynecology?
A. It is a special branch of sports medicine that focuses on the special medical needs of the woman athlete.

Q. How will I know what progress I'm making during my swimming program?
A. On the following page, chart your progress during the postpartum period.

Q. Where can I find the swim gear you've discussed in the book?
A. Branches of *Mothercare* and shops in the *John Lewis Partnership* usually stock maternity swimwear. However, most good sports shops should also be able to help you find something suitable.

35

Family and Baby Swim Q's

Q. Why should my baby be taught water skills and swimming?
A. There are several reasons to introduce your baby to water skills. First, learning and practicing these skills will help him to develop his strength, coordination, and motor skills. Second, when properly exposing him to the water at an early age, you are helping him develop important water safety skills and a love of and confidence in the water. Third, he'll have a great time playing in the water. And finally, you'll have a great time teaching him and watching him develop.

Q. Can you suggest some guidelines to help me introduce my child to the water?
A. First, *never, ever* let your child near water without appropriate supervision.

It's most important to introduce your child to the water gradually so that he will feel secure and will learn to love and respect the water.

Remember always to kiss, smile, hug, and applaud your baby for his accomplishments.

(Bonus: After a swim, both you and your baby will sleep well!)

Q. Can a baby really learn to swim?
A. Few if any children can really learn a basic swimming stroke before

the age of three. However, younger children can learn basic skills such as breath holding, turning over in the water, rudimentary paddling, floating, holding on to the side of the pool, and entering the pool from the side. These skills, if properly taught, may save a child's life if he accidently enters a body of water.

Q. What kind of swimming facility is appropriate for a baby?
A. First of all, the pool should be clean, warm, well-maintained, and protected by the proper use of chlorine and other additives. There must be an area for your child where he will not be exposed to collision with other swimmers or rough water. Water and air temperature should be warm so that your baby will not get chilled. Under optimum conditions, it is best to have a shallow area where your child is able to stand up.

Q. What kind of safety skills should I know before I take my baby into the pool?
A. You should know how to swim competently so that you are adept and at ease in the water. You should know CPR (cardiopulmonary resuscitation) and mouth-to-mouth resuscitation, and how to properly use a life jacket and other flotation devices.

Q. What should I do if my baby swallows water?
A. If your baby swallows some water and coughs or sneezes to clear his throat, don't worry. Just let him bring up the water if he wants to. Of course you must always be ready to administer mouth-to-mouth resuscitation or other first aid in the event that it's needed.

Q. Can my baby contract an ear infection or other sickness from the water?
A. Babies are susceptible to ear and other infections, but it's not likely that your baby will contract an infection from the pool water if the pool is properly maintained and his ears are carefully dried after swimming. One way to help remove any water remaining in the ear is to gently suction baby's ear by turning him to one side as you place your palm over it and press lightly. Also you could use a blow dryer on a warm setting to dry the water.

Of course you should never take your child into the water if he's sick or suffering from an ear or eye inflammation or upper respiratory problem. By the way, avoid using ear drops or eye drops on your child, unless they are prescribed by your pediatrician.

Q. What should my baby wear in the pool?
A. Your baby should be dressed in cloth diapers (not disposable diapers, which inevitably disintegrate in the pool) covered with rubber pants that fit snugly around his waist and legs (in case of accident). He may also wear a T-shirt in the water for warmth.

Q. What should I take with me when I take my baby to the pool?
A. You should bring a large towel, a robe with a hood to keep your baby warm, extra diapers, and some plastic bags for storing wet items. Bring some powder or lotion to help prevent chapping.

Q. Is there any danger to my baby, or myself, from the chlorine in the pool water?
A. No. The chlorine, if properly used, is quite safe for your baby and you. Chlorine helps to protect your baby's health (and your health) by killing bacteria and algae and causing matter such as perspiration, suntan lotion, and other pool contaminants to break down.

Q. How can flotation devices be helpful?
A. Flotation devices can include tubes, water wings, and styrofoam inserts in bathing suits. They are most helpful when they allow the child to move freely and practice swim skills. They are most useful in open water for safety. Everyone should wear a life jacket or P.F.D. (personal flotation device) in water crafts.

Be sure not to rely on flotation devices for safety. Use flotation devices with discretion, and remember that your child must always be supervised when using them.

Q. What are the benefits of the sink-or-swim method of teaching my child to swim?
A. Nothing positive can be gained from the sink-or-swim method. Never hold your child under the water, or allow him to flounder in the water. In fact, if unscheduled dunkings occur with any frequency, your child may become apprehensive of the water, and you may lose his trust.

Q. What action should I take in the event of a swimming accident?
A. If the victim is not breathing, it is imperative that you help the victim obtain oxygen *without delaying – seconds are precious.* You can learn artificial respiration through your local St. John's Ambulance Brigade or at your swimming pool. Follow this procedure in an emergency:

Clear the victim's airway by turning the victim face up and opening his throat by placing a hand under his neck and gently lifting while tilting his head backward with the heel of your palm against his forehead. Insert your fingers into his mouth, clear away any foreign matter, and move his tongue if it is obstructing his throat.

If the victim does not immediately commence to breathe on his own, take a deep breath, pinch the victim's nose, cover his mouth with your mouth, and breathe into his mouth to force air into his lungs. If the victim is a small child, instead of pinching his nose, cover both his nose and his mouth with your mouth. Release your mouth from the victim, inhale, and repeat. Breathe four times for the victim, checking to see that his chest inflates.

If it does not, check the victim's airway for obstructions. Listen and feel for the exhalation of air by the victim. If the victim does not resume breathing by himself within ten seconds after you have commenced your resuscitation efforts, continue to breathe for him until his breathing is restored or help arrives. You should breathe twenty times per minute (once every three seconds) for a child and breathe twelve times per minute (once every five seconds) for an adult. Check for the victim's pulse as soon as you commence resuscitation efforts. If you cannot detect a pulse, you should attempt cardiopulmonary resuscitation if you have been trained in the technique. Of course as soon as you learn of an accident you should attempt to obtain medical assistance.

Q. When the baby is old enough, and I decide to start him or her swimming, is there any way to keep a check on his or her progress?
A. Yes. Use the following chart to record your baby's swims.

FOLLOW YOUR BABY'S SWIMS

Date/Baby's Age	Baby's Height & Weight	Water Location	Time in Water	Water Play/Swim Skills	Special Comments/Baby's Reaction

Index

Index

Abdominal muscles, 4
Alternate breathing, 111
Ankle stretches (exer.), 75
Answers to common questions, 225-37
Aquae Sulis, 6
Aqua jogging (exer.), 80-81
Arm and leg stretch (exer.), 81
Arm circles (exer.), 64
Arm motion, 15, 16
  catch, 15
  pull, 15
  recovery, 15
  S-shaped, 16
Arm presses (exer.), 63-64
Arm works/swim salute (exer.), 65
Arteries, 6
Artificial respiration, 236-37
At-home Waterworks, 57, 86-90
  bathtub and shower, 87-90
  bobbing, 86
  effleurage, 87
  equipment, 86
  feet flex, 88
  Kegel, 89-90
  pelvic tilt, 88
  shoulder shrugs, 88
  sink or washbasin, 86
  sitting leg bends, 87-88
  tailor press variations, 87
  tailor sit, 87

Babies. *See* Infants; Family swimming; Newborns
Baby's swim chart, 238
Back kicking (exer.), 73
Back massage (exer.), 72
Backstroke, 30-38
  arm exercises, 35-36
    pop-up, 36
    stretch to stand, 36
    treading, 36
    windmill catch-up, 36
  benefits of, 37-38
  body position, 30
  breathing, 30-31
  breathing exercises, 37
    rapid chest, 37
    transition, 37
  elementary, 31-32
  leg exercises, 36-37
    alternating kicks, 37
    free kicking, 37
    sit and kick, 36
    wall kick, 37
  push-off, 47
  sculling, 31
  skills, list of, 30
  tips on, 37-38
  turn, 49-50
  variations, 30
  windmill, 34-35
Ballet leg position (synch.), 193-95
Ballet leg submarine, 194-95
Ballistic movement, 99
Bathing caps. *See* Caps
Beauty care, questions on, 230
Bicycle pedal (exer.), 74

Blood supply, 5
Bobbing (exer.), 80
  at home, 86
Body and hip press (exer.), 68-69
Body position, 13-14, 15
Body roll (crawl stroke), 18
Breast-feeding, 232
Breasts, size during pregnancy, 4
Breaststroke, 23-29, 32-34
  arm exercises, 28
    stroke count, 28
    walking, 28
  arm motion, 23-25
  benefits of, 29
  body position, 23
  breathing, 26-27
  breathing exercises, 28-29
    cleansing breath, 29
    early labor technique, 29
  coordination, 27
  frog kick, 25
  inverted, 32-34
  leg exercises, 28
    kickboard kick, 28
    sit and kick, 28
    vertical kick, 28
    wall kick, 28
  leg motion, 25-26
  push-off, 47
  tips on, 29
  turn, 49
Breathe and reach (exer.), 58-59

Breathing and bobbing (exer.), 59-60
Breathing patterns used during labor and delivery (exer.), 60-61
   chart, 62
Breathing Waterworks, 58-62
   bobbing, 59-60
   breathe and reach, 58-59
   cleansing breath, 58
   head circles, 59
   labor and delivery breathing patterns, 60-61
   chart, 62
   rhythmic breathing, 60
Breathing with head circles (exer.), 59
Broad ligaments, 4
Buddy system, 96
Buoyancy, 13
Butterfly stroke, 204-6
   arm motion, 204-5
   breathing, 205
   coordination, 205
   dolphin kick, 204, 205
   double arm backstroke, 205-6
   leg motion, 205
Byron, George Gordon, Lord, 6

Calf stretches (exer.), 75
Caps, 96
   Latex, 96
   Lycra, 96
Cardio-aerobic fitness, 2-3
Catch, defined, 15
Cesarean section, 8, 163
Childbirth, 8-9, 57
   Lamaze technique, 8-9
   Leboyer technique, 8
   Waterworks and, 57
Children. *See* Family swimming

Chlorine, 229, 236
Circle position (synch.), 196-97
Circle spray (exer.), 68
Clam, 193
Cleansing breath, 43-44, 57n., 58
   Waterworks exercise, 58
Contraction and relaxation movement, 99
Coordination, 15
Crawl stroke, 16-22
   arm exercises, 19-20
   catch-up stroke, 19-20
   S-shaped pull, 20
   stroke count, 20
   arm motion, 16-17
   benefits of, 21-22
   body position, 16
   body roll, 18
   breathing, 18
   breathing exercises, 21
   walking and, 21
   wall kick and, 21
   coordination, 18
   flutter kick, 18
   leg exercises, 20-21
   breathe and kick, 21
   kickboard kick, 20-21
   prone wall kick, 20
   sit and kick, 20
   leg motion, 18
   push-off, 47
   tips on, 21-22
   turn, 49
Crouch position dive, 203

Dick-Read, Grantly, 9
Diet, 3, 228
Diving, 202-3
   crouch position, 203
   head-first, 202
   semi-standing, 203
   shallow sitting, 202-3
   standing, 203

Dolphin circle, 196-97
Dolphin kick, 204, 205
Double arm backstroke, 205-6
Double ballet legs, 195
Double leg circles (exer.), 78
Duct figures (synch.), 199

Ear infections, 235
Effleurage
   defined, 57
   as exercise, 85
   at home, 87
Elementary backstroke, 31-32
   arm motion, 31
   coordination, 32
   leg motion, 32
Equipment, 96-98, 232
   purchasing, 232
Exercise during pregnancy, myths about, 5
Exercise program. *See* Waterworks exercises

Family swimming, 209-22, 234-38
   artificial respiration, 236-37
   baby's swim chart, 2
   benefits for children, 209-10
   chlorine, 236
   ear infections, 235
   flotation devices, 236
   as ideal activity, 209
   infants, 213-16
   newborns, 211-12
   preschoolers, 220-21
   questions and answers on, 234-38
   safety, 210
   sink-or-swim method, 236

INDEX

swallowing water, 235
toddlers, 217-19
youngsters (ages six to teens), 222
Fartlek conditioning, 132
Feet flex (exer.), 88
Fins, 51, 97
Flamingo ballet leg submarine, 195
Floating with safe recovery (exer.), 82
Flotation devices, 236
Flutter kick, 18
Focal relaxation (exer.), 84-85
Foot circles (exer.), 78
Foot-first vertical, 197
Frog kick, 25

Goggles, 96-97
Gynecology, 232

Hand paddles, 97
Hang ten (exer.), 65
Head-first diving, 202
Head-first vertical, 197-98
Health, questions on, 238-40
Hemorrhoids, 5
Hot tubs, 226
Hula-Hoop hip rotation (exer.), 69-70
Hydrotherapy, 6

Infants, 213-16
 bobbing with, 214
 cuddling, 214
 floating, 215
 holding on to pool edge, 215-16
 paddling and kicking, 215
 passing baby between adults, 215
 security feelings, 213
 submerging, 214-15
 water environment, 213
 See also Family swimming
Interval swimming, 107
Inverted breaststroke, 32-34
 arms, 33
 coordination, 33-34
 legs, 33

Jacuzzi tubs, 226

Kegel (exer.), 89-90
Kennedy, John F., 6
Kickboards, 50-51, 97
Kicking variations
 dolphin kick, 204, 205
 flutter kick, 18
 frog kick, 25

Lamaze childbirth technique, 8-9
Lamaze tailor sit (exer.), 79
Layout position (synch.), 190-92
Leander, 6
Leboyer childbirth technique, 8
Leg and inner thigh extension (exer.), 74-75
Leg bend and stretch (exer.), 81
Leg lifts (exer.), 69, 76
Leg motion, 15
Leg roll, 191
Leg scissors (exer.), 74
Leg swirls (exer.), 77
Lochia, 163
Logs. *See* Personal Swim Log (chart)
Lower back pain, 4, 226
Lower body Waterworks, 73-79
 ankle stretches, 75
 back kicking, 73
 bicycle pedal, 74
 cald stretches, 75
 double leg circles, 78
 foot circles, 78
 Lamaze tailor sit, 79
 leg and inner thigh extension, 74-75
 leg lifts, 76
 leg scissors, 74
 leg swirls, 77
 lower leg stretch, 77
 medley of kicks, 73-74
 tiptoe stretch, 75
 wall walk, 78
 wide knee bends, 75
 water ballet barre exercises, 75-76
 water Kegel, 78-79
Lower leg stretch (exer.), 77

Marching step, 194
Marlin turn, 191-92
Medley of kicks (exer.), 73-74
Medley of pulls (exer.), 63
Medley of strokes, 44
Menstruation, 231
Middle body Waterworks, 68-72
 back massage, 72
 body and hip press, 68-69
 circle spray, 68
 Hula-Hoop hip rotation, 69-70
 leg lifts, 69
 pelvic rock, 71
 pushing, 71-72
 sit-ups, 70
Movement, principles of, 13-14
 body position, 13-14
 buoyancy, 13
 Newton's Third Law of Motion, 14
Myths about pregnancy, 5

Newborns, 211-12
 bathing with, 212
 baths, 211-12

INDEX

water play, 212
water temperature, 211
See also Family swimming
Newton's Third Law of Motion, 14

Olympic pools, 98

Pace clocks, 97
Passive movement, 99
Pelvic girdle, 4
Pelvic rock (exer.), 71
Pelvic tilt (exer.), 88
Pendulum body swing (exer.), 82-83
Personal Swim Log (chart)
  baby's swims, 238
  first trimester, 115
  postpartum, 233
  second trimester, 140
  third trimester, 159
Physical conditioning, 2-3
Pike position (synch.), 193
Pike's pull (exer.), 84
Plank, 199
Pools, 97-98, 219
  wading pools for toddlers, 219
Postpartum program, 163-211, 231-33
  abdominal surgery, 163
  breast-feeding, 232
  butterfly stroke, 204-6
  C-section delivery, 163
  described, 164
  diving, 202-3
  introduction to, 163-65
  lochia, 163
  menstruation, 231
  Personal Swim Log (chart), 233
  questions and answers on, 231-32
  synchronized swimming, 164, 189-202

  tips on, 164-65
  twelve-week program, 166-88
  vaginal infection, 231-32
  week 1, 166-67
  week 2, 168-69
  week 3, 170-71
  week 4, 172-73
  week 5, 174-175
  week 6, 176-77
  week 7, 178-79
  week 8, 180-81
  week 9, 182-83
  week 10, 184-85
  week 11, 186
  week 12, 187-88
Posture check (exer.), 84
Pregnancy
  abdominal muscles, 4
  blood supply, 4
  bodily changes during, 3-5
  breast size, 4
  cardio-aerobic fitness, 2-3
  center of gravity and, 4
  childbirth, 8-9, 57
  chlorine and, 229
  colds during, 228-29
  diet and, 3, 228
  hemorrhoids, 5
  lower back pain, 4, 226
  myths about, 5
  pelvic girdle, 4
  physical conditioning for, 2-3
  postpartum program. *See* Postpartum program
  skin and hair care, 230
  sun exposure and, 230
  swelling in lower extremeties, 5
  swim program. *See* Pregnancy swim program
  urination, 226
  uterus, changes in, 4

  vaginal infection, 229
  varicose veins, 5, 229
  vitamins, 228
  water breaking during swim, 226
  Waterworks exercises, 55-90
  weight gain, 3
Pregnancy swim program, 93-159
  ballistic movement, 99
  buddy system, 96
  comfort, importance of, 93
  contraction and relaxation movement, 99
  courtesy, 98
  equipment, 96-98, 232
  finding swimming facilities, 99
  frequency, 96
  intensity, 96
  introduction to, 93-99
  length of program, 94-95
  main swim, 93-94
  passive movement, 99
  progression, 96
  purpose of, 94
  reminders, 99
  safety and, 98
  schedule, 95
  slow progressive stretch, 99
  starting, 93, 95
  stretching and, 99
  stretch-out, 93-94
  three-part sessions, 93-94
  tips, 93-94, 98, 99
  trimester 1, 100-15
  trimester 2, 116-40
  trimester, 3, 141-59
  warm-ups, 93
Preschoolers, 220-21
  diving for pennies, 221
  proper swim

INDEX

techniques, 220
"train and engineer", 221
"whale ride", 221
See also Family swimming
Pull, defined, 15
Pull buoys, 97
Pushing (exer.), 71-72
Push-offs, 47-49
  backstroke, 47
  breaststroke, 47
  crawl stroke, 47
  sidestroke, 48
  tips on, 48-49
Pyramid swim, 118

Questions and answers, 225-38

Recovery, defined, 15
Rhythmic breathing (exer.), 60
  at home, 86
Roman baths, 6
Roosevelt, Franklin D., 6

S-shaped arm motion, 16
Safety
  pregnancy swim program and, 98
  questions on, 228-30
  tips on, 9
Scissor kick, 42
Sculling
  defined, 31
  synchronized swimming and, 190
  as Waterworks exercise, 65-66
Semi-standing dive, 203
Shallow sitting dive, 202-3
Shark circle, 196
Shoulder shrugs (exer.), 88
Side kick and touch (exer.), 81-82
Sidestroke, 39-45

arm exercises, 42-43
  combination pull, 43
  unders and over, 42-43
arm motion, 41-42
benefits of, 44-45
body position, 39
breathing, 40
breathing exercises, 43-44
  cleansing breath, 43-44
cordination, 42
leg exercises, 43
  bicycle pedal, 43
  kickboard kick, 43
  trudgen kick, 43
  wall kicking, 43
leg motion, 42
medley of strokes, 44
push-off, 48
scissors kick, 42
starting position, 41
tips on, 44-45
top arm recovery variation, 42
trudgen crawl, 44
turn, 50
variations, list of, 39, 44
Sitting leg bends (exer.), 87-88
Sit-ups (exer.), 70
Slow progressive stretch, 99
Spas, 6
Sports gynecology, 232
Standing dive, 203
Stroke-count, 108
Stroke Cues Chart, 46
Strokes, 13-51, 190, 204-6
  arm motion, 15
  backstroke, 30-38
  basics, review of, 15
  body position, 13-14, 15
  breaststroke, 23-29, 32-34

breathing, 15
butterfly, 204-6
coordination, 15
crawl, 16-22
Cues Chart, 46
leg motion, 15
medley of, 44
movement, principles of, 13-14
push-offs and, 47-49
review of, 13-15
sidestroke, 39-45
synchronized swimming variations, 190
turns and, 49-51
Swallowing water, 235
Swelling in lower extremities, 5
Swim fins, 51, 97
Swimming
  advantages over other exercise, 7
  arterial health and, 7
  artificial respiration, 236-37
  at-home Waterworks, 57, 86-90
  backstroke, 30-38
  benefits of, 3-5, 6-7
  as best exercise, 6
  breaststroke, 23-29, 32-34
  breathing Waterworks, 58-62
  butterfly stroke, 204-6
  childbirth and, 8-9
  chlorine and, 236
  crawl stroke, 16-22
  diving, 202-3
  equipment, 96-98, 232
  families, tips for, 209-22
  finding facilities, 99
  heroic feats and, 6
  interval, 107
  introduction to, 1-10
  lower body Waterworks, 73-79

middle body
    Waterworks, 68-72
movement, principles
    of, 13-14
personal comments on,
    1
pools, 97-98
postpartum program,
    163-206
pregnancy swim
    program, 93-159
push-offs, 47-49
questions and answers,
    225-38
safety tips, 9, 98,
    228-30
schedule for, 7-8
sidestroke, 39-45
Stroke Cues Chart, 46
strokes, 3-51
synchronized (water
    ballet), 164,
    189-202
three times a week, 7
total body Waterworks,
    80-85
turns, 49-51
upper body
    Waterworks, 63-67
water, 5-7
Waterworks exercises,
    55-90
weight control and, 3
See also Pregnancy
    swim program
Swimming gear. *See*
    Equipment
Swimsuits, 96
Synchronized swimming,
    164, 189-202
    ballet leg position,
        193-95
        double ballet legs,
            195
        flamingo ballet leg
            submarine, 195
        matching steps, 194
        submarine, 194-95
    circle position, 196-97

dolphin circle,
    196-97
shark circle, 196
defined, 189
duet figures, 199
    plank, 199
    water wheel, 199
layout position, 190-92
    log roll, 191
    marlin turn, 191-92
music and, 189
pike position, 193
    clam, 193
sculling, 190-200
stroke variations, 190
tandem strokes, 200
team swimming,
    199-200
tuck position, 192
    tuck turn, 192
vertical position,
    197-98
    foot-first, 197
    head-first, 197-98
    "V" leg split, 198
workout, 201-2
Synchronized swimming
    workout, 201-2
    figure and stroke
        combination, 201-2
    main swim, 201
    stretch-out, 202
    stroke skills, 201
    warm-up, 201

Tailor press variations
    (exer.), 87
Tailor sit (exer.), 87
Team swimming
    (synch.), 199-200
Tiptoe stretch (exer.), 75
Toddlers, 217-19
    blowing bubbles
        underwater, 218
    "magic slide" for,
        218-19
    repetition and, 217
    wading pools for, 219
    water play, 219

Total body Waterworks,
    80-85
aqua jogging, 80-81
arm and leg stretch, 81
bobbing, 80
effleurage, 85
floating with safe
    recovery, 82
focal relaxation, 84-85
leg bend and stretch,
    81
pendulum body swing,
    82-83
Pike's pull, 84
posture cheek, 84
side kick and touch,
    81-82
treading water, 83-84
Towel stretch, 102
Transition breathing, 156
Treading water (exer.),
    83-84
Trimester 1, 95, 100-15
    bobbing, 101-2
    breathing, 101
        and bobbing, 102
    entering the water, 101
    highlights, list of, 100
    knee bends, 102
    on-deck sitting, 101
    Personal Swim Log
        (chart), 115
    tips on, 101-2
    towel stretch, 102
    wall flutter kicks, 102
    warm-up skills, 101
    week 5, 103
    week 6, 104
    week 7, 105-6
    week 8, 107
    week 9, 108
    week 10, 109-10
    week 11, 111-12
    week 12, 113-14
Trimester 2, 95-139
    highlights, list of, 116
    Personal Swim Log
        (chart), 140
    week 13, 117

INDEX

week 14, 118-19
week 15, 120-21
week 16, 122-23
week 17, 124-25
week 18, 126-27
week 19, 128-29
week 20, 130-31
week 21, 132-33
week 22, 134-35
week 23, 136-37
week 24, 138-39
Trimester 3, 141-59
  breathing exercises, 141
  changes in routine, 141
  discomforts during, 141
  highlights, list of, 142
  Personal Swim Log (chart), 159
  week 25, 143-44
  week 26, 145-46
  week 27, 147-48
  week 28, 149-50
  week 29, 151
  week 30, 152
  week 31, 153
  week 32, 154
  week 33, 155
  week 34, 156
  week 35, 157
  week 36, 158
Trudgen crawl, 44
Tuck position (synch.), 192
Tuck turn, 192
Turns, 49-51
  backstroke, 49-50

breaststroke, 49
crawl stroke, 49
sidestroke, 50
tips on, 50-51

Upper body Waterworks, 63-67
  arm circles, 64
  arm presses, 63-64
  arm works/swim salute, 65
  hang ten, 65
  medley of pulls, 63
  sculling, 65-66
  wall push-ups, 66-67
Uterus, changes in, 4

Vaginal infection, 229, 231-32
Varicose veins, 5, 229
Vertical position (synch.), 197-98
Vitamins, 228
"V" leg split, 198

Wading pools, 219
Wall push-ups, 66-67
Wall walk (exer.), 78
Water, 5-7
  curative history of, 5-6
  hydrotherapy, 6
  need for, 5
  Roman baths, 6
  spas, 6
Water ballet. *See* Synchronized swimming
Water ballet barre exercises, 75-76
Water jets, 98
Water Kegel (exer.), 78-89
Water wheel, 199
Waterworks exercises, 55-90
  at-home, 57, 86-90
  benefits of, 56
  breathing, 58-62
  childbirth and, 57
  defined, 55
  five categories of, 56
  lower body, 73-79
  middle body, 68-72
  in stretch-outs, 55-56
  tips on, 56-57
  total body, 80-85
  upper body, 63-67
  using, 55-56
  in warm-ups, 55-56
Weight control, 3
Wide knee bends (exer.), 75
Windmill backstroke, 34-35
  arms, 34
  legs and coordination, 35
  S-pull variation, 35

Youngsters (ages six to teens), 228